SAFE AT LAST
A Handbook For
Recovery From Abuse

David J. Schopick, M.D.
with Suzanne Burr, Ph.D.

WATERFRONT BOOKS
Burlington, Vermont 05401

Cover illustration by Colleen McLaughlin
Cover Design by Lisaius Marketing
Typography by Bold Face Type and Design

Printed in the United States by Daamen, Inc.

Library of Congress Cataloging-in-Publication Data

Schopick, David J., 1955-
 Safe at last: a handbook for recovery from abuse / by David J.
Schopick.
  p. cm.
ISBN: 0-914525-28-x (cloth)
    0-914525-27-1 (paperback)
1. Adult child abuse victims. 2. Cognitive therapy. 3. Sexual abuse
victims. 4. Psychological abuse. 5. Self-help techniques. I. Title
BC569.5.C66538 1995
616.85'822390651 dc20   95-19355
                                                   CIP

This book is dedicated to
my children, Ben and Adam,
and to my wife Gail.

Contents

The Serpent: The Monster of Sexual Abuse

The Chameleon: The Monster of Rejection

Part 3 Steps to Recovery

Part 4 Healing Techniques & Exercises

Introduction

If you have picked up this book and are reading this page, then you know better than I how abuse has affected your life. Perhaps you were a victim, or perhaps a friend or family member was. Whatever your reason for being drawn to this book, I hope you will find in its pages a portion of the strength and hope you are looking for.

As a psychiatrist in private practice and as a hospital staff member, I have had the opportunity to work with many children, teenagers, and adults who are struggling to overcome some kind of abusive past. Some have had a parent who inflicted the wounds of verbal abuse through harsh, persistent scolding and blame. Others have been beaten or physically assaulted. And some have suffered the terrible abuse of sexual molestation or incest. A growing number of the patients I see also are dealing with more subtle forms of abuse which are only recently receiving more attention in the media. I'm referring to the abuse caused by rigid and unforgiving social ideas, such as racism, sexism, and homophobia.

The statistics back up my personal experience that there is a crying need for resources to help people in recovery from abuse. For example, at present we know that at least one third of all women and one sixth of all men under the age of 18 have been sexually abused. That is a cruel reality.

I wrote this book because I wanted to share a concept that has worked well for my patients and which I believe may be helpful for you. I use the image of the monster, or beast, as a way of talking about the process of abuse. Basically, when abuse occurs, it is as if the abuser has a harsh, critical monster or beast sitting on his (or her) shoulder. Through the process of the abuse—whether it is verbal, physical, sexual, or cultural abuse—the monster leaps from the shoulder of the abuser to that of the victim. Unless there is some kind of intervention in the form of new awareness or therapy, that monster can stay on the shoulders of the victim forever.

Perhaps you may already feel that this is true for you. If that is so, I would like to offer you some hope. That monster can be dislodged, and a new vision of your own inner goodness and wholeness created to take its place. The metaphor of the monster, or beast, gives you a visual symbol to help simplify the recovery process. It makes it much easier for you to tackle the next step: getting rid of the monster, along with the shame and guilt that has accompanied it for years.

The concepts in this book have been used successfully with patients of both sexes and of all ages, from an 11-year-old boy to a 69-year-old woman. I hope they will work for you too. If you are in treatment now, I hope the book will enhance what you and your doctor, or your group, are working on. If you are not in therapy, I hope you will find the book a helpful guide and support as you courageously overcome the past and learn to heal.

About This Book

This book is written as a handbook for you to use as a support in your recovery and healing. It's not meant to interfere with your current treatment but to enhance it. This book is a personal resource. It doesn't use a lot of psychological jargon. In simple terms, it tries to help you understand how abuse affects you, how it can make you think and feel.

The book is divided into 4 parts. In Part 1, I explain the basic concepts of the "The Monster on Your Shoulder," including the goal of such therapy, and how it grows from what we call cognitive therapy healing by understanding how people's thoughts affect how they feel and what they do. I describe what a "monster" is and show how it works as a legacy of abuse. Part 1 also presents an approach to healing that addresses key issues such as responsibility, power and powerlessness, and stages in personal growth.

Part 2 is real-life stories which provide several examples of "monsters on the shoulder." These examples run the gamut from personal conflicts to larger social issues of racism, sexism, and homophobia. Chief kinds of abuse dealt with here are perfectionism and inhuman expectations; verbal abuse; sexual abuse; and extreme rejection.

This section is not a definitive collection of the many different kinds of monsters that can exist. Rather, it shows some typical mental beasts that many survivors struggle with. I tell these particular stories to give you hope. Many of the people I write about conquered the harsh, critical monsters on their shoulders. You can do it too.

Parts 3 and 4 are your handbook for healing. Part 3, "Steps to Recovery," outlines some of the issues you will likely confront as you heal. I begin by focusing on courage since I fervently believe that courage is the chief quality possessed by people in recovery. I have been impressed again and again with the bravery, persistence, and sheer "heart" of people with whom I've worked. And since one of the greatest challenges to one's courage is learning how to trust again, that challenge is also covered here in Part 3.

In Part 3, I also discuss some of the different types of therapy: psychotherapy, group therapy, and family therapy. I present an overview of the different medications that are sometimes prescribed for patients, and talk about some of the pros and cons of using them. The last topic explores a therapist's potential "monsters," and how to make sure you are getting the good help you deserve when you choose treatment.

Part 4 includes practical tips on a wide range of techniques you can practice whether or not you are in treatment. These techniques have helped people cope with emotional ups and downs and are especially useful to survivors of abuse.

Major topics in Part 4 include relaxation exercises, such as controlled breathing, meditation, visualization, and self-hypnosis. A variety of enjoyable exercises with writing and art are also included. You can use these to free up your creative inner voice, express your feelings, evoke memories that may need to be dealt with, and give yourself an outlet during the rough moments of life.

Writing a letter to your monster or to your abuser (without the intention of mailing it) can be especially empowering. In this form of writing therapy, it is as if the writer's arm becomes a slide, and the monster slides from the victim's shoulder onto the paper. Once the monster of abuse is on the paper, the victim can more clearly see the monster for what it is: a creature that belongs to the abuser, not the victim. I have been amazed at the speed with which survivors can work through their issues and reconnect with old memories and emotions when they use this method.

Techniques for better communication are also a major focus in Part 4 since many abuse survivors are helped by learning more assertive ways of dealing with conflict and asking for what they need out of a relationship. Teaching you to think like a strong survivor rather than a victim is the goal of the four chapters on communication.

All these exercises, tips, and techniques form a kind of "beast-busting portfolio." The techniques may be especially useful if you are under great stress, dealing with painful issues in therapy, or confronting old wounds from the past. These techniques can also be used throughout your life for greater self-mastery and serenity.

Finally, there is a chapter on forgiveness, which can be a healing balm for many survivors.

Though I hope you will find the idea of "monsters on your shoulder" compelling and helpful, there are many other resources available to you as you continue to heal. At the end of the book, a Resources section tells you about books and organizations. Pick and choose the ones that will serve you best. And never lose heart. You and you alone have the power to be master of your heart, mind, and soul. The challenge is to summon all the supports and inspirations you can find as you move forward on your journey.

Ultimately, no monster is strong enough to triumph over your inner strength. That's what this book is all about.

Acknowledgments

This book and my achievements are like the top of a pyramid with thousands of people underneath. These people, to whom I owe so much, form the all-important foundation of knowledge, support, motivation, experience, and love.

Nine years of medical training provided by hundreds of dedicated instructors and mentors taught me to appreciate the power and specialness of the physician-patient relationship.

At the University of Pittsburgh, I received wonderful training in modern general and child psychiatry. Prominent faculty members shared their knowledge and expertise with residents and fellows.

My mentors included Carol Anderson in Family Therapy, Ted Petti in Community Psychiatry, Alan Axelson in private practice, and Maria Kovacs in Cognitive Therapy. Maria, whom Aaron Beck has called "the godmother of cognitive therapy," was my supervisor. She taught me about motivating and encouraging patients. From David Kolko in Behavioral Therapy I learned how to break down the seemingly overwhelming task of therapy into small manageable steps. Joaquim Puig-Antich in Pharmacology helped me to appreciate the benefits of medication while recognizing its limitations, an approach you will find in this book.

After medical school, residency, and post-doctoral work, came clinical practice, and the opportunity to learn from colleagues and patients. I feel a special debt of gratitude toward the patients who shared their lives and suffering with me. Working with both children and adults allowed me to see the effects of abuse at various developmental stages, and to share these insights with patients of all ages.

I am fortunate to have worked with some very courageous people. Some of my most courageous patients have been children and teens. It takes enormous courage and trust for these young people to begin the necessary work towards recovery. I hope that if you are a teenager, or if you are the parent of a child or adolescent, you will find this book helpful.

The seeds of this book grew slowly from all the aforementioned influences, but there were also several special "sparks" along the way. Sheila Bethel-Muarray, a world-renowned motivational speaker, has been an inspiration. I heard her speak at the New England Speakers Association conference in 1991. That day she emphasized that, as a public speaker, you reflect what you truly care about. I knew then that for me, that issue was child abuse.

Another motivational speaker whose words have touched me deeply is Zig Ziglar, whom I heard at a lecture he gave in Portland, Maine. In his lecture to over two thousand sales professionals (and one psychiatrist), Ziglar focused on values and quality of life. I realized that he was practicing very high quality Cognitive Therapy. I left that session with tips and metaphors that could be used to help people change the way they think. Ziglar's comments on forgiveness also became an important touchstone in my approach to therapy; I include one of his wise sayings in the final chapter of this book.

The Stepwork of Alcoholics Anonymous played a major role in my developing approach to abuse, to control issues, and to acceptance of human limitations. For over three decades the "monkey on the back" image has been used in the recovery community as a metaphor for addiction.

For example, a patient of mine recalled a memorable remark that he heard at an AA meeting: "When you put down your drink and get the monkey off your back, it doesn't die; it goes in a corner and eats bananas. If you pick up the next drink, it's back on your back, but this time it's King Kong." AA used the monkey metaphor to talk about the damaging cycle of addiction.

My own search for images that would simplify the concepts of how abuse transmits self-hatred and blame from one person to another eventually led me to the use of stories and myths in therapy, and the development of the "monster" metaphor.

The monster is different for everyone. Its face changes according to the unique background, personality, issues, and expectations of the person who has experienced abuse. For some people the monster is a vicious, critical bird of prey; for others it's a seductive serpent or snake. The metaphor is particularly compelling for those who have gone through physical or sexual abuse. For these individuals, it's almost as if their abuser, a real-life monster, is sitting on their shoulder now, weighing them down with shame and guilt.

This book is for all of the people who fight against these mental monsters, for the therapists and especially for the brave and tenacious patients who have allowed me to share their struggles and triumphs.

Great appreciation is due Suzanne Burr, Ph.D. Her background is that of a talented literary writer. It is her contribution to the organization and flow of the book that has made it so readable.

A special note is due Dr. Jerry Storm of Exeter, New Hampshire. Jerry is a behavioral pediatrician who taught me how to be a real doctor. His genuine love of people, especially children, has been a continual inspiration. He has opened my eyes to the spiritual side of medicine and life in general. Our profession needs mentors like Dr. Jerry Storm to encourage the best in its young doctors. I know that his contribution to my own life has been immeasurable.

It is to Jerry Storm, my mother, my late father, my wonderful and loving wife and children, my siblings, my teachers and mentors, and all my patients, that I dedicate this book.

David J. Schopick, M.D.
Portsmouth, New Hampshire

Part 1

You and Your Monsters

1

Buddha and the Beast

In a story once told about Buddha, a man asks Buddha whether or not he is required to accept abuse when another man is abusive. Buddha asks the man, "To whom does a gift belong if the intended recipient refuses the offer?"

The man thinks about it. Then he says, "Why, it remains the property of the giver."

Just because someone hands you abuse, you don't have to accept it.

Buddha then asks, "Why should it be any different with abuse?"

Like all enlightened beings, Buddha grasped a simple truth. *Just because someone hands you abuse, you don't have to accept it.* Yet thousands of years later, many of us still struggle to understand this basic fact.

Understanding how abuse happens, how and why it hurts, and how you can move beyond it is what this book is all about.

2

The Face of the Beast

Picture someone walking into a room. On the person's shoulder is a monster. That monster represents all the "baggage" the person has accumulated over the years. It comes in all sizes and wears many faces.

It may be anger at life, rage at unfulfilled hopes and dreams.

It may be perfectionism, the refusal to accept human limitations.

It may be the desperate need to be loved, admired, or placed on a pedestal.

It may be the need to help or save others, or the need to be followed and hailed as a great leader.

The point is, that person is not free. The monster is always there, yammering into his ear, shaping every interaction.

Have you ever met someone who gave you the feeling you were supposed to forgive them for something? Perhaps you have a friend who is always apologizing. Maybe she keeps asking for your approval in a hundred different ways. It may be that your friend is sporting a very large monster of shame which makes it difficult for her to feel good about herself. That monster has made your friend dependent on others for her self-esteem. As long as your friend is held hostage to her monster in this way, she can never be totally free to love herself or others.

When a parent or loved one verbally abuses a child, or when a child is battered or sexually molested, a vicious monster is transferred from one person to another. Often, the abusive parent is in a great deal of pain, and this pain, too great for the parent to bear, is inflicted on the child instead. It is as if a copy of the beast is created, which then leaps from the abuser's shoulders onto the child's shoulders.

In this way, the abuse is internalized by the child: the brutal monster becomes a part of him. This can happen even if the abuse lasts only a few seconds. It doesn't take abuse repeated over a period of years for the process to be set in motion, nor is it limited to interactions between parent and child. If an event is traumatic enough, it can have an enormous impact on a person's life, regardless of their age.

What kind of monster might you be carrying around as a result of verbal or physical abuse?

If it was physical abuse, it might be the monster that says, "Violence is love." The monster that says, "You deserve to be hit (or yelled at, or mistreated)". Or the one that says, "All you're good for is as a punching bag."

If it was verbal abuse or harsh criticism, it might be the monster that says, "You're bad" or "You're weak."

If it was sexual abuse, you may have the monster that says, "All you're good for is as a sexual object." Or a monster that says, "Your sexual feelings are dangerous," "You're sinful," or "Sex is dirty."

No matter who delivers it, abuse of any kind is not love!

If it was neglect, or unreasonable expectations, or denial of your worth as a person, your monster may be constantly chattering that "you're worthless," or that "you don't deserve respect," or "you're unloveable."

If you have been abused as a child, it is vitally important that you reject these monsters and place them where they belong: squarely on the shoulders of the abuser, whether it be your mother, father, sibling, loved one, or stranger. No matter who delivers it, abuse of any kind is not love!

Abuse is an act of selfishness and self-centeredness. Sometimes confronting this fact brings an enormous sense of loss. Recovery may require establishing greater emotional distance from the people who have hurt you. It may mean letting go of a beloved image and admitting that the same person who loved you also hurt you very deeply. But this work is crucial, if you are ever to be free of "the monster on your shoulder."

3

The Goal of Monster Therapy

In the previous chapter, you learned to picture an abuser as someone with a terrible monster on his or her shoulders. When abuse happens, the abuser gives you, the victim, a copy of the monster. It then sits on your shoulder and stays there indefinitely. If there are several abusers, or many instances of abuse, you may have a collection of monsters on your shoulder, an entire "monster zoo."

The goal of Monster Therapy is for you to learn to identify when there is a monster, what kind of monster it is, and who really owns it.

Cognitive Therapy is the science of the way people think, and how that affects the way people feel. Monster Therapy could be viewed as a type of Cognitive Therapy. It uses the monster image to help simplify the recovery process, to help you visualize how abuse has affected your mind, that is, how abuse affects the way you think, and then, how that affects how you feel.

By identifying the type of monster you carry around as a result of the abuse, or "naming the beast," you can learn to free yourself from its stifling grip on your thoughts and emotions. You can learn to say, "No, that monster is not mine, and I refuse to accept it."

This is especially important if you are a survivor of childhood abuse.

A child who is abused emotionally, physically, or sexually is not able to reject what is happening. It is very rare for a child to be able to say to a parent or loved one, "That's your problem, not mine." Since a child usually depends upon and looks up

> You can learn to say, "No, that monster is not mine, and I refuse to accept it."

to the adult, the child almost always accepts the abuse (the monster) and takes on the monster as his own. If this happened to you, you probably grew up thinking the abuse was your fault.

Now, as a teenager or adult, you have an amazing opportunity: to see the abuse for what it really was. You can learn to see the abuse as the other person's problem or monster, not your fault or personal failure.

Childhood abuse is an extreme example of what happens in human relationships. Even when we have grown out of childhood, our challenge in life is to learn how to keep people from abusing us, to keep them from giving us their monsters. We need to understand how human interactions work and how to set firmer boundaries around our hearts and minds. We also need to recognize when the monster is our own and then take responsibility for it.

By grasping these basic concepts and by exploring the techniques presented later in this book, you can learn how to reject other people's attempts to place their monsters on your shoulders.

> You probably grew up thinking the abuse was your fault. You can learn to see the abuse as the other person's problem or monster.

You can learn how to put up mental defenses to defend yourself, whether from a subtle annoyance or a downright assault on your self-esteem. If you are in recovery from childhood abuse, you can gain a better understanding of how that abuse occurred, and how to free yourself from its crippling grasp. It's a matter of learning new ways of listening, interpreting, speaking, loving, and living.

Let's take an example from the movie, *"The Karate Kid."* The young man, Daniel, has finally convinced Mr. Miyagi, martial arts master, to teach him karate. Daniel's first lesson is to paint an enormous fence. But not just any old way. He must do it with one brush in each hand, alternating between hands with precise strokes. Daniel paints the huge fence.

Next, Daniel must wash Mr. Miyagi's cars. Again, he must follow a precise method, using circular motions of both hands. Daniel gets a bit irritated, but he performs the tasks without objection. By the tenth car, he's fed up. He demands that Mr. Miyagi explain the value of this labor. (Daniel is losing trust in his instructor.) Mr. Miyagi answers with a mock attack on Daniel. Using the hand movements he learned while painting the fence and washing the cars, Daniel responds automatically to Mr. Miyagi's fierce karate maneuvers. Suddenly, the purpose of his labor becomes clear and Daniel's faith is restored.

Monster Therapy is like this process, too. The monster metaphor is designed to help you gain some insight into how abuse passes from one person to another. Monster Therapy involves teaching yourself new ways to think and feel, and new ways to respond to others' gestures and the "monsters" they may want to thrust upon you.

Anybody can do it. I've seen this concept work for patients of all ages, from an 11-year-old boy to a 69-year-old woman. You don't need special skills. You don't need to be a Buddha or a Mr. Miyagi. But you do need to know who really "owns" the abuse and how to reject it before it can hurt you.

Learning to identify the abuse as monsters can be like changing the prescription of your glasses in order to see more clearly. Looking through the new lenses, you'll be amazed at the number of monsters you recognize now that you can see them.

4

Abuse and the Beast (or The Battered Wife Syndrome Made Simple)

Have you ever wondered why abuse appears to run in families, why abused children so often grow up to become abusers themselves? It is because the pain and rage becomes a part of that child's psyche. Abuse victims can spend their whole lives seeing the world through the eyes of enormous overgrown monsters that live on their shoulders 24 hours a day.

You may ask, why do children accept these monsters from their parents?

As I mentioned before, the reality is, that's what kids do. They don't know how to screen abusive talk or behavior because this is all they know. They don't know what is abuse and what is not abuse. The monsters that occur in an abusive home are particularly confusing because there are so many. By the time a child is a teenager, he or she has become accustomed to a parent's abusive comments. Abuse has cemented a harsh, critical beast on that child's shoulder. Without understanding, without outside help, a child grows up to live under the weight of that cruel monster forever.

The dysfunctional family is a breeding ground for monsters, where parents put responsibility for their own failures and disappointments onto their children, as their own parents or guardian may have done to them. Sometimes it is in the form of verbal abuse. This kind of abuse is extremely damaging, leaving scars that can last a lifetime. In some cases, the frustration from failure and disappointment takes even more sinister forms of physical or sexual abuse.

Why do some people seem to seek out abuse, even when they see it destroying their lives?

If you have experienced abuse, it's important to know exactly how it has affected you. In my experience working with hundreds of patients, I find that abuse is probably the most effective way to harm a person's self-esteem. Trauma can have a major influence on the development of the personality. It can forever damage the way a person relates to others.

Why do the effects of abuse linger so long? Why do some people seem to seek out abuse, even when they see it destroying their lives?

To answer these questions, let me share a personal story with you.

One sunny day during the summer of 1991, I was watching my two sons as they played in the backyard of our home. At that time, Ben was four and a half, and Adam was two and a half. At one point I had to go inside the house to look for something. Keeping a close eye on the kids through the window as I searched, I saw Ben all of a sudden hit Adam. Naturally Adam started crying. I think we have a pretty healthy family (we work at it!), but still, at that age, Ben could sometimes get pretty aggressive toward Adam.

Anyway, I didn't immediately go to comfort Adam and break things up. Instead I kept on looking for what it was I needed in the house. When I glanced up again, what I saw stopped me in my tracks.

Adam, still crying, was wrapping his arms around Ben. He was hugging him, and Ben was hugging him back.

That's when I finally understood "The Battered Wife Syndrome" or, in this case, "The Battered Brother Syndrome."

Adam was hurt. He needed comforting. The only one available to comfort and nurture him was the very person who had harmed him: his abuser.

I learned some important things that day. One is that within families, abuse is not "just" abuse. It usually includes seeking and accepting nurturance from the very people who also harm you.

This is probably the most humiliating part of the abuse cycle in families. The perpetrators often provide the comfort and the "love". This coupling of abuse and nurturing can be particularly intense for incest survivors. I suddenly understood why it is so difficult for many victims of longstanding abuse to walk away from bad relationships. The pain is welded to the love.

Why bring this up now? Because if you are struggling to come to terms with childhood abuse,

Abuse usually includes seeking and accepting nurturance from the very people who also harm you.

the first step is recognizing that having warm and loving feelings for those who have harmed you is not sick. It is understandable and normal under the circumstances.

Even more important, it is normal for children to feel responsible for things that happen in their lives. It may seem like a paradox, but that is how self-esteem is built. When good things happen, the child feels responsible. Her self-esteem grows. You might say that instead of a monster, she has a proud creature, a glowing, winged bird, on her shoulders.

But when bad things happen, the same rule applies. This is so common as to be a universal principle. So it is very human and understandable to feel that the abuse was somehow your fault. But it was not!

A final note to this story: after the incident with my sons, I made some changes in my own family. I decided that I would do all I could to teach my children not to seek nurturance from people who have harmed them. I don't want my sons to learn that abuse and nurturance go hand in hand. This requires vigilance because sometimes the abuse can occur with friends.

I also decided that when I get upset and treat my children abruptly, I don't want to turn right around and hug them and "lay on the nurturance." That would be teaching them that hostility and caring go together. Rather, I have to ride out my guilt (my own monster).

Knowing that I can't "absolve myself" of guilt by suddenly becoming "Mr. Nice Guy," has made me more thoughtful in my initial reaction and even more determined to behave more respectfully and positively toward my children and others.

5

Learned Powerlessness

Most people find it hard to deal directly with their anger. Culturally, we believe anger is bad, dangerous, or uncivilized. We try to find ways to cope with angry or painful feelings, and sometimes this means shutting them off altogether or even denying they exist at all.

It's natural for people to dislike pain. Pain hurts. But in severe trauma, it goes far beyond this and can evolve into Learned Powerlessness. In Learned Powerlessness, an abused person learns that getting angry is dangerous. Getting angry can invite more abuse or rejection. Fear of that causes the person to keep quiet and subsequently feel powerless. Instead of responding to aggression by getting angry and showing it, the person freezes up. Eventually the person equates anger with powerlessness. Anger, as one might normally think of it, is transformed into silent inaction.

I see this especially among victims of abuse. If you were abused as a child, you learned that you have no control over your body, your mind, your privacy, your life. You probably felt enormous anger and humiliation, but there was little you could do about it. In fact, often the only thing you could do was comply, and then bury your anger and pain.

The result is you learn that when you are angry and hurt, you do nothing. You become paralyzed. Over time, you learn to behave this way in most relationships and situations whenever you are angry or hurt, regardless of the reality of the situation. Even if you were to tell someone who would be quite open to your anger—a loving spouse, a

If you can't feel and express anger directly so that it can be resolved, you stifle your capacity to experience your own strength and self-mastery.

supportive therapist, or sympathetic friend—you probably still wouldn't be able to let yourself feel or express your own anger. As a result, you have no sense of personal freedom and power. If you can't feel and express anger directly so that it can be resolved, you stifle your capacity to experience your own strength and self-mastery.

Many women who were abused as children describe how they complied with unwelcome sexual advances because they were incapable of saying no. They learned this sense of powerlessness as children over time. They were not born with it.

You may have had a similar experience. Abuse can damage your sense of personal power so badly that you are more vulnerable than average to exploitation in your present-day life.

Violent behavior in children can sometimes be a sign of extreme powerlessness. Take the case of Sally, a 10-year-old who had been hospitalized because of her violent behavior. In the hospital, Sally seemed sweet and gentle. But at home, when she became angry, she attacked. She once went after her mother and brother with a butcher knife. This gentle girl punched holes in walls and tore up furniture. On many occasions, the police had to be called just to control her.

Once we had hospitalized Sally, we began to understand her more deeply. It turned out that when Sally was two, her biological father had abandoned her, and she hadn't seen him since. Shortly before being admitted to the hospital, she called him on the phone. In spite of having not heard from him for eight years, Sally had high hopes. But her father needed a moment before he remembered that he even had a daughter. He was cold and distant, and Sally felt totally crushed.

Sally revealed some of her other problems too. She began to talk about physical abuse at the hands of both parents, but especially her stepfather. She recalled a series of incidents when she felt mocked, humiliated, and rejected by him. She felt that her mother did nothing to prevent it. In fact, Sally's mother took her husband's side, and Sally wound up feeling completely alone and abandoned.

During Sally's first family session, both her mother and stepfather were present. Knowing Sally's background, I hoped that she would express how much she feared and hated her stepfather, perhaps even tell about specific times he had hit her or verbally abused her. I hoped that she would tell her parents how painful it was to have been blamed by her stepfather for getting chicken pox on the day of his marriage to her mother. Or that she would talk about how hurt she was when her stepfather encouraged her brother to tell the kids at school that she was a bed-wetter. He would tease her and call her "Peepot," a name that enraged her.

But Sally just couldn't speak up. She got out a few muffled words, then went silent. I call this "hitting the wall." Sally could go no further because she had run into an invisible barrier in her mind that stopped her from speaking about her extreme pain.

The next day I asked Sally about "hitting the wall," her inability to express her feelings toward her stepfather. She admitted that the reason she was so hurt by her stepfather's blame on his wedding day was that she had wanted him to like her. She feared that grievances against him now could actually jeopardize any chances of his liking her.

In reality, Sally was simply a 10-year-old kid who had been abandoned by her biological father and who desperately wanted her new "father" to like her. But she had no idea how to get close to him. To make things worse, Sally didn't know what to do about his abusive style. She felt powerless in his presence, and so she went mute just when she needed words the most.

At the time, I felt that unless Sally confronted her stepfather and worked through all these issues, she would run the risk of getting involved in unhealthy, even abusive, relationships with men in the future. All too often, abuse victims gravitate to people who are like their abusers.

Later you'll find out what happened to Sally. For now, I want to emphasize that Sally's story is not unique. Many victims continue the pattern of abuse because of the emotional paralysis (Learned Powerlessness). The cycle continues unless the victim learns to confront the pain and develop a sense of mastery over such relationships.

The image of a beast or monster serves to represent the terrible damage abuse does to many people. Fear of confronting an abuser causes the victim to hold back angry, painful feelings that remain with the victim as a sort of beast that repeatedly hurts the victim. Anger that needs to be directed at the abuser instead turns inward at the victim.

In extreme cases, this unresolved anger can lead to suicidal thoughts or acts. Sometimes the first move in treatment is to establish safety, to protect the victim from his own monster so that the healing process can begin.

This was the case with one patient, Robert. A 35-year-old man with a history of depression, Robert had attempted suicide many times in the past and had been hospitalized twice. He had tried several different psychiatric medications with no apparent benefit. I was reluctant to prescribe further medications because of his chronic suicidal thoughts and the risk of his attempting an overdose.

Also, in his case, since we both feared it would foster an unhealthy dependence, hospitalization did not appear to be a good option either. I spoke with Robert openly and honestly about my concerns. I explained that I wanted to try to help him with the tools that I had available to me as a physician, but I was afraid that he might overdose. Robert became annoyed, arguing that it wasn't fair for me to deprive him of a medicine that might be helpful. He argued eloquently that he had always phoned me whenever he felt intensely suicidal and said he would accept any recommendation to be hospitalized.

I agreed to try new medications on an outpatient basis. Before I gave him the new prescription, I told him that if he were to attempt suicide with the medications that I prescribed for him, I would interpret that to mean he was very angry toward me.

Robert thought that was the most absurd thing that he'd ever heard. But I was firm in making it clear to him that I believed there would be a close tie between his suicidal behavior and his immediate feelings about me. The tipoff would be if he tried to kill himself with the medications that I had prescribed. A few weeks later, he became very angry one night and began pouring the medication into his mouth. He intended to overdose and die. Later he told me that as he was doing this he thought about my warning that a suicide attempt like this would indicate that he was very angry at me. It dawned on him that this was indeed the case. With that, he concluded, "Schopick's not worth it!" and spit out the drugs. Robert had finally realized that he had been taking his anger toward others and turning it onto himself in a very lethal way. The monster he had been carrying around was turning on him. By spitting out the drugs, he took an important first step in redirecting his anger. Far better that he direct his anger at me, who knew how to channel and use it to his benefit, rather than at himself. Though anger at others was not the ultimate goal of Robert's therapy, it was a first step in breaking the cycle of self-hatred. His throwing the monster at me was a step before throwing the monster off his shoulder altogether.

The goal of this book is to help you recover that personal power which you may have lost as a result of abuse.

Recovering from abuse (emotional, physical, or sexual) involves learning how to take back control over your life. Recovering personal power is not easy. But developing a clear perception of your personal monster or beast can help a great deal.

It's different for everybody. Your monster will have its own unique size, shape, color, and voice. The ultimate goal is confronting the beast so you can get free of it. When you can experience this sense of self-awareness, you are on the path to self-confidence and recovery. Instead of carrying your abuser's monster on your shoulder, you can learn to toss it off and take back something that belonged to you all along, your self-respect.

6

Who's Got the Monster?

An important legacy of abuse is the way in which it may damage a person's ability to perceive reality. In particular, it can blur the lines of personal responsibility. After all, when a parent "crosses the line," violating a child's dignity (in the case of verbal abuse) or body (in the case of physical abuse), a child becomes confused. She tries to understand what is happening to her. To make sense of it, she may identify with her abuser and deny the pain she causes herself or others. That's what makes monster mayhem so insidious.

After recognizing which monsters belong to your parents or to other abusers, it is also important to recognize which monsters belong to you, and where your personal responsibility begins.

Let me give you an example. A patient of mine I'll call Carol suffered from a severe form of Bulimia-Nervosa, an eating disorder which is a combination of Anorexia Nervosa and Bulimia. For Carol, eating was a traumatic event. When I first began working with her, she would almost always vomit after eating a meal. As a result, Carol's health and very life were in danger.

Where did this beast come from? Carol had been raped by her father when she was thirteen years old, and since the age of seven had been sexually abused by an older brother. As Carol and I explored this painful past, we discovered that the vomiting had a precise cause: swallowing food triggered flashbacks of performing fellatio with her brother.

Through the course of therapy, Carol made progress. One day, however, I made a mistake. I threatened a feeding tube if she did not reach a certain weight by a particular time. She said nothing, but simply stopped eating altogether. The next day she came into my office and looked me square in the eye.

"Dr. Schopick, I want to tell you that it's all your fault."

"What's all my fault, Carol?," I asked. I had a hunch what was coming.

"I'm not eating, and it's all because of what you said to me. See what you've done!"

Well. Carol's monster leaped toward me like a leopard with sharp claws. It's true I had made a mistake, but I was not the cause of her eating disorder. I told Carol that while I apologized for my error, I refused to accept the monster, namely, her belief that starving herself and derailing her treatment was my fault.

I reminded her where the beast really came from: her father and brother when she was a child. More important, the beast was now hers to deal with and disarm. I pointed out that she was using self-injury as a way to get even with someone she was angry with, rather than talking it out and venting her feelings. I also pointed out that she now had choices she didn't have as a child.

Carol's example demonstrates several important lessons of Monster Therapy: taking responsibility

> **R**ecovery isn't about transferring your monster to somebody else. It's about doing the inner work to free yourself so that the monster loses its power to hurt you.

for your actions now, while understanding the impact of the abuse; identifying personal inner beasts and monsters and dealing with them without having to foist them off onto other people; not accepting monsters that belong to others.

Recovery isn't about transferring your monster to somebody else. It's about doing the inner work to free yourself so that the monster loses its power to hurt you. The reward for doing away with "beastly business" and accepting personal responsibility is improved quality in your relationships with others and with yourself.

I once worked with a courageous teenage boy named John whose father had abandoned him nine years earlier. In our work I tried to help John learn how to start dealing with his feelings, especially his feelings of loss. John seemed to be grasping the concept of the therapy well, and so I asked him to try writing a letter to his father. John said he would, and he took pen and paper in hand to start the process.

Ten minutes later he reported he had written "nothing." Actually the paper was not blank. John had doodled while we spoke.

> The point is, when you reject the monster,
> rather than rejecting yourself or others,
> you're moving forward to recovery.

What did his drawings show? Did he draw a picture of himself killing himself or his father?

Not at all. The first drawing was of a monster sitting on a young man's shoulder. The monster had sharp horns and the end of its tail was shaped like a spear. Superimposed over the monster was a circle with a line through it (the international "no" symbol), signifying John's utter rejection of his monster.

A second drawing showed a monster with fangs and horns. The inscription below it said, "Kill the Monster."

John had taken an important step.

The point is, when you reject the monster, rather than rejecting yourself or others, you're moving forward to recovery.

The remainder of this book explores a number of healthful approaches you can use to free yourself, through traditional treatment and innovative self-help methods, and presents life-stories of other people who have coped with a monster on their shoulder. Perhaps you will recognize yourself in some of the stories that follow.

Part 2

Life Stories

The Harpie:
The Monster of
Expectations

7

You Must Have It All

Have you ever looked at a newborn's feet and hands?

Minutes after his birth, I remember looking down at my baby son, cradled gently in his mother's arms, and thinking that this is a perfect being. At that moment, my firstborn looked so beautiful to me, I trembled. I know in my soul I would have felt that way no matter what my baby actually looked like. It was the perfection, the complete oneness and originality in its broadest sense, of that baby that took my breath away. Here was a completely new human being.

It's the same way with a child's mind. At the moment of birth the child is wrapped in a kind of perfection that comes from a divine place: God, if you are religious; the Unknown Perfection, if you are not sure what lies beyond this world. Whatever the source, the spirit of a child at birth is whole. Untouched. Open to the world. Perfectly ready for whatever life has to offer. Even babies born with debilitating afflictions like Fetal Alcohol Syndrome or HIV have a spiritual perfection that comes from their moment of pure arrival into the world.

One of the hardest things for most of us to grasp about life is that we will never be this perfect again. In a way, life seems like a regression from the perfect state that heralds our beginnings. We grow older and become marked by the world, by our parents, our friends, our family, our work partners, even the physical environment. We begin to acquire hurts and fears, shame and guilt. Our bodies change, losing the resilience of youth, or succumbing to disease.

We also grow in positive ways, making choices: a job, a spouse, a child. But even good changes alter us forever. We move ahead, as we must, as the imperfect beings that we are, unable to ever again regain that moment of perfection at birth.

Many people cannot accept the basic fact of our human existence that we are not perfect. They seem to live as if they, their children, their loved ones, and friends could achieve perfection. As a culture we seem to accept this pursuit of perfection. Striving for better, smarter, and more is the mark of goodness and virtue. Popular messages promise, "You can be it all, have it all."

We want the perfect body, the perfect mind. Consider the advertisements that suggest to women, "You must look like this model, be a certain weight, color your hair to be loved and respected." The commercials say to men, "You must have this car to be happy." Witness our obsession with SAT scores and grade point averages, our ranking of children in school as though they were horses in a race for absolute intelligence.

I remember how when I was in grade school we called ourselves "A students," "B students," "C students," and so on. The grade became a symbol for our value as human beings instead of a rating of certain skills.

Is it then any wonder that the recent television show about Barney, the kind purple dinosaur, has become so popular with children? This show, of modest beginnings, turned into a runaway hit that astonished parents, educators, and television executives. Who is Barney, after all? A loving, all-accepting parent figure whose theme song is "I love you, you love me, we're a happy family!" Barney is a friendly purple monster children can take inside themselves for nurturing and comfort.

Parents are responsible for the messages they send to their children. Think about some of the expectations that may have been conveyed to you when you were young. Were you expected to be successful in business, when what you really wanted was to be a singer? Were you pushed to excel in sports when you craved to curl up with a good book and dream the hours away in your imagination? Were you scolded for your sexual feelings when inside you was a passionate, sensual person whose deepest longings were for love and romantic connection? I'm sure you can think of ways in which your parents, family, and friends may have said to you, either directly or indirectly, "You are not enough just as you are. You should be what WE want you to be, not what YOU want to be."

Perhaps you were raised in an environment where no matter what you did, you felt it would not be enough to satisfy your parents, make them love you, praise you, nurture you. I often see this syndrome in children who were abused or who grew up in alcoholic or other kinds of dysfunctional families.

If this is so, you probably have a strong and determined monster on your shoulder which now repeats all the old sayings about your inadequacies, your failure to "make the grade." I call this monster the Harpie, after the mythological winged bird that preys on people.

This creature can be a killer. I have seen minds and lives nearly destroyed by monsters (Harpies) that make the development of normal self-esteem impossible. To me, the Harpie represents a monster on the shoulder that "harps" on another person's flaws or foibles. In a sense, this monster won't let another person just be themselves. It constantly harps on the things the person could do better, should do better, or would've done better "if only you'd listened to my advice."

Let's look at a few of these Harpies in action.

8

Be Just Like Me

If sons look to fathers for how to be men, it's also true that many fathers see images of themselves in their sons. However, the image is not of who the father really is, but rather who the father aspired to be. Through the father's eyes, the son is no longer himself but is instead a potential example of a smiling, handsome, successful individual.

If, instead, Father sees a frustrated, unhappy, stifled face staring back at him, he becomes frightened and desperately wants to change what he sees. The son becomes the vehicle for the father to change all the things about himself he hates. The result is monster mayhem.

Take the case of Bobby who is 11 years old and a child of divorced parents. His biological father was physically abusive to him while his parents were married. Although that form of abuse ended with the marriage, the problems, however, did not.

The trouble started with a simple game of baseball. A man of some athletic prowess, Bobby's father, John, had hoped to someday break into the major leagues. That had been his dream, and he had given it his best shot. Unhappily for him, he did not have the level of skill required. And so the dream died.

But not quite. It started to come alive again when Bobby turned ten. Whenever John talked to Bobby, he would pressure him about baseball. He urged Bobby to join Little League, and quoted statistics about batters and pitchers, averages and

The son becomes the vehicle for the father to change all the things about himself he hates. The result is monster mayhem.

runs until Bobby was numb. Then John would throw out little monster-barbs like, "What's the matter? Isn't baseball good enough for you?" or, "You know how important this is to me! How can you let me down like this? Can't you even try, just once!"

Bobby's mother noticed that whenever he returned from a visit with his father, Bobby was angry, even enraged. Bobby just didn't like baseball. Plain and simple.

The baseball diamond was being turned into a battlefield. John had turned his own thwarted ambition into a monster that was riding him. Unable to let it go and move on to another dream, he placed his monster, the unfulfilled wish for achievement in baseball, onto Bobby's shoulders. The result was that Bobby felt angry and anxious whenever he and his father got together. He began to loathe his father for pressuring him to play baseball.

What would Bobby do when his father placed these monsters on his shoulders?

Nothing.

That is, nothing in his father's presence. But when Bobby returned to his mother's house after one of these visits, he became verbally abusive to his mother and stepfather and physically aggressive with his two younger sisters. Do you see the process? Because he feared his father and feared losing his father's love, he did not stand up to him and, figuratively, allowed his father's monster to control him. When he got home where he felt safer, he dumped his anger, the monster, on everyone else, behaving aggressively toward his loved ones.

To complicate matters, Bobby suffers from asthma and his attacks are very distressing both to him and to people around him. Whenever Bobby was attacked by his father's monsters, the asthma attacks got worse.

When Bobby came to see me as a patient, I explained Monster Therapy to him and his mother. Bobby had a tough time understanding it conceptually, but his mother became my ally and co-teacher. Two days after I gave Bobby and his mother their first lesson, Bobby phoned to tell me he had told his father he did NOT enjoy playing baseball with him. What a victory!

John had become enraged and threatened never to see him again. Bobby and I talked about how rigid his father was in this instance, essentially demanding the right to place very unfair monsters on Bobby's shoulder any time he felt like it. Fortunately, Bobby knew his father wasn't serious about his threat to never see him again. He stood firm and didn't cave in to his father's manipulation.

Bobby learned an important lesson that day. By not accepting his father's monster, he didn't feel anywhere near as depressed and angry as he used to when there was a blow-up with John. He was becoming more aware of the monsters as if they were really visible.

He also noticed something else. His asthma subsided a bit during this episode. Bobby realized that the asthma attacks were less of a problem when he didn't take on his father's monsters! Young as he was, Bobby achieved a key insight. It turned out that his asthma was aggravated by anxiety. Anxiety resulted when Bobby felt anger at his dad. No monsters, no anger, less asthma.

Several months later, while Bobby and his mother were talking to me about "the happiest day in our lives," Bobby informed his mother that the happiest day in his life was when he used Monster Therapy on his father.

Working with Bobby and his mother taught me how valuable the parent can be as co-therapist or co-teacher. I also learned that young children can learn and apply this concept just as well as adults. In fact, Bobby learned and applied it faster than most adults with whom I've worked.

9

Don't Make My Mistake

If you think fathers and sons are a tough combination, it is said that the mother-daughter connection is even more fraught with dangers and pitfalls.

Perhaps that is one reason why Nancy Friday's classic was so popular. It must have touched a chord in thousands of women who saw the intimate connection between their own identities and their mother's.

> Young girls look to their mothers for confirmation of what it means to be a woman. And mothers often look to their daughters for confirmation of their own self-worth and success.

Young girls look to their mothers for confirmation of what it means to be a woman. And mothers often look to their daughters for confirmation of their own self-worth and success. It's a devilishly hard relationship for many women to figure out because the mirroring is so complex. Where does the mother leave off and the daughter begin?

Many of my patients are only able to deal with their own monsters after they have recognized and understood those of their mothers. Only then can they see what kind of messages about femininity have been handed down to them.

Take the case of Joanna.

Joanna's mother, Sarah, was a sensitive, artistic woman. Sarah suffered severe post-partum depression after Joanna was born and had to be hospitalized. During her hospitalization, Sarah received electro-shock therapy. It was a terribly painful episode for the whole family.

When Joanna was growing up, Sarah would warn her about having children. She would say over and over again, "You'd better be careful, because when you grow up and have a baby, the same thing will probably happen to you." In other words, "Don't make my mistake!" Sarah was subtly implying that "you'll regret having a child." "If you have a child, it will be a disaster," and even, "You're unwanted." Sarah wasn't talking about a genetic predisposition to post-partum depression; she was talking about being unworthy, and of being "destined" to be a failure as a mother. Sadly, Joanna believed these messages. After all, her childish logic told her that this was her mother talking, and she should know.

Joanna's father made it worse by telling her in a very cynical way that "all girls grow up to be just like their mothers." There were now two monsters settling firmly into Joanna's heart and mind.

For years Joanna believed these monsters, but she buried her fears in all the activity of growing up and leaving home. After graduating from college, Joanna married; in a few years she had her first child. Almost immediately after giving birth to a baby girl, Joanna found herself stricken with terrible thoughts, thoughts like, "I've really done something awful." "Only pain will come of this." "I really messed up." Joanna found it hard to enjoy the pleasures of her new baby, and was afraid to take her daughter home from the hospital.

Do you recognize the monster at work here? Since childhood, Joanna had been carrying around a monster that told her having children would bring ruin to her and her family. It revealed itself at the moment when Joanna's and her mother's life paths finally crossed in shared motherhood. What should have been a wonderful experience was turning into something of a nightmare for Joanna as it had for Sarah years earlier.

Fortunately, Joanna spoke to her obstetrician. She assured her that post-partum depression was not "catching." By getting the information and support she needed, Joanna freed herself from the monster that said motherhood was dangerous.

Sons and daughters, fathers and mothers, we are all talking a mythic language of monsters as we transmit our feelings onto one another. As you'll see in the next story, this is especially true during the "white water rapids" of adolescence.

10

A Is the Only Grade

We talk about the "terrible two's" but what about the "terrible teens"?

Adolescence can be a time of incredible turmoil. It's often a time when a child's body begins to mature, and the child experiences a myriad of feelings never known before or experienced as deeply: sexual feelings, but also feelings about friendship, goals, work, and the future. It's also a time when all the expectations of society and family hit especially hard. The pursuit of perfection becomes a strong desire to fit in, be normal, be one of the guys, be liked, be special.

Teens in abusive homes have an added burden and they usually find ways to soften the pain. This can take the form of escape (through drugs, alcohol, food), acting out (rebellion, risky behavior, hurting others in the same way), or other kinds of defensive actions. Because of the serious consequences that can result, the actions themselves and the attendant consequences become yet more monsters that the teen must face. Even if the home is not abusive, teens can be at risk because of the pressures they feel inside themselves and from society in general. Usually these fears focus on their ability to take their place in the world. No wonder a hallmark anxiety for teens is an obsession with academic achievement.

This was the case with one of my patients, a young man named Phil.

Phil was a perfectionist. He was so much of a perfectionist that when he got anything less than an A in high school, he became deeply depressed. Unlike many teens, Phil did not have a history of abuse. Furthermore, his parents didn't pressure him to perform well in school. Phil suffered from a serious psychiatric illness that expressed itself in an extreme need for academic achievement. To Phil, anything less than an A meant he was a failure as a person. He had no core of self-esteem to ride him through being merely "good" or "okay" in school. It was so painful for Phil to do less than the best that several times when his grades went down, he actually tried to kill himself. That's how deep the pain went.

Luckily, Phil's parents got him into treatment, and through a combination of psychotherapy and medication, Phil was able to recover from his severe depression. Although medication was clearly a major factor in his recovery, I also taught him the concepts of Monster Therapy to help him understand how his mind worked.

The monster model helped Phil see that his unreasonable beliefs about academic success were destroying his life. He had bought into all the cultural messages, society's myth, about what good grades mean. Phil's perfectionistic streak around school was a vicious monster on his shoulder. It yelled in his ear, "You're so stupid! You can't do anything right!"

While doing well in school leads to increased self-esteem, an over-reliance on grades for their own sake becomes destructive.

I believe that Phil's example is an extreme case of what many teenagers feel on a daily basis. The lesson we can learn from Phil is this: while doing well in school leads to increased self-esteem, an over-reliance on grades for their own sake becomes destructive. Parents can help teenagers weather this storm by placing academic success in a broader picture of overall health and happiness.

The myth at the core of our culture, that we can "have it all" in every way at every moment leads to incredible stress and turmoil and, in some cases, to physical illness. We must come to terms with our unrealistic expectations of ourselves and others. By accepting our limitations we can look this monster in the eye and refuse to accept its harsh, unrealistic and inhuman expectations.

The Vulture:
The Monster of
Verbal Abuse

11

It's All Your Fault

Picture a vulture swooping down on its innocent victim. Slowly it circles in the sky, waiting for just the right moment to attack. When it sees the victim weakening, the vulture makes its move. It tears at the flesh of its prey, glutting itself.

Verbal abuse is like a vulture that gnaws away at a person's mind. When a child experiences verbal abuse, such as repeated criticism, blame, anger, or shaming, he or she can internalize those words. In many cases the words become a part of the child's conscience forever. The child grows up thinking, "I am bad," or "It's all my fault." Then he acts out this myth of himself the rest of his life, finding or creating situations where he is rejected or unloved.

Because they are going through so many changes, teenagers are also very vulnerable to verbal abuse. Often the teen years are when all the family myths and monsters that have been buried in the child's psyche or the family's collective memory may emerge from their lairs and cause havoc.

Take the case of Mark, a 14-year-old boy. When Mark was 6, his 3-year-old brother died in a drowning accident. Mark was very fond of his younger brother, and his death was a terrible loss. What made the situation almost unbearable was that Mark's grandfather blamed him for the accident and told him so. The grandfather's wounding words sank deep. Mark absorbed his grandfather's words of shame and torment. He bought the myth that his brother's death was his responsibility.

Mark lived for years with this awful monster on his shoulders. He believed that if anything went wrong in any situation, it was his fault. If people in the street glanced his way, they were glaring at him for something he had done wrong. If a waiter in a restaurant forgot his order, it was because the waiter could see Mark was a terrible person who didn't deserve to be treated well. If a girl at school didn't send him a valentine, it meant she hated him. And on and on.

In his therapy, Mark and I strove to identify the monster that had been gripping his shoulder like a vice for so many years. Mark saw that the monster came from the awfully hurtful things his grandfather had said to him about his brother's death. So Mark did a very brave thing: he decided to write letters to his grandfather.

In these letters, Mark poured out the pain that had been bottled up inside him for more than seven years. He expressed his deep hurt and unhappiness, telling his grandfather how terrible he felt about being blamed for his brother's death. He described the torment of not only losing a much-loved brother, but feeling that he'd lost his grandfather's love, too. He wrote that sometimes he had felt so guilty that he wished he had died instead of his brother.

These letters were very helpful, not for the effect on his grandfather, but rather for the transformation that took place inside of Mark's mind and soul. As Mark wrote these letters and confronted the very painful memories, he realized that the blame for his brother's death was not his. Mark had been a mere child of six years old! When his brother died, it was an accident, just that, an accident, not someone's fault. When Mark gained this insight, he understood that as a young child he had not been able to identify false accusations and defend himself against them. But it was not too late now and, over time, he learned how to reject abusive monsters.

12

Take A Message

Family guilts and unhealed wounds are not the only family monsters that can plague children and make the teen years a living hell. Divorce, now so common in our society, is a very troubling event for youngsters. It can be even harder for older children because they see and understand more of the subtle tensions.

Children are often caught in the middle of divorce. Many times when this happens, it is a result of parents using a child as a go-between or messenger between them. Between warring parties, the child becomes the monster messenger, as it were. Tragically, though, the messenger gets hurt in the process. When parents talk through a child, the parent sending the message may intend the nasty words (the monster) to land on the other parent. Unfortunately that parent doesn't realize that the child in the middle is hurt by those words, burdened by the nasty words monster clutching the child's shoulder.

Let's take an example. Say a mother who is getting divorced feels strong resentment because her child support payments are smaller than she'd hoped, and she has to get a second job. During the divorce she may drop little comments to her daughter, such as, "I really wanted to quit my job and go back to school. I guess I'll have to work even harder now that your father has snowed the judge."

The mother intends this verbal tidbit to get passed along to her ex-husband. Maybe the message gets through, maybe it doesn't. But what's absolutely sure is that the daughter has gotten the message loud and clear. The mother is sending a "blame telegram" to her child. This only builds on

> It is far healthier to learn how to stay out of the middle than to deliver messages back and forth between two people who play Kill the Messenger!

a bad situation, since children tend to feel divorce is their fault anyway.

Unless there's some kind of intervention from a family member or other adult, the daughter will most likely begin to see her father as a selfish, greedy person. Thus the monster message that was intended for the father really takes a different victim, the child.

My advice to children or teens in this situation is to learn how to identify the monsters and then reject them. I encourage children of all ages to tell their parents that it is not their monster, thank you very much, and that they won't deliver the message. Maybe the sending parent will get annoyed at them for this stance. But it is far healthier to learn how to stay out of the middle than to deliver messages back and forth between two people who play Kill the Messenger! Kids need to see this game for what it is: a kind of abuse.

13

Hear My Laughter,
Feel My Pain

One of my favorite examples of humor as pain occurred with a teenage girl I once treated. She spoke rapidly and changed thoughts quickly. I had to race to keep up with the lightning-speed transitions of her mind. But as we worked together, I began to notice that within her rapid pace and changing ideas were subtle, almost unnoticeable insults, rather snide offhand remarks meant to pass as jokes.

While others laughed off her brashness and rudeness, it became clear to me that her humor was neither pleasant nor complimentary. Rather, it was quite abusive. She was so quick at dishing out her insults that at first all I was aware of was an annoyed feeling. Eventually, I began to realize what she was doing. She had been verbally abused by parents who had shamed her and made her feel inadequate. They had hurled their monsters at her, and now she was doing the same with me, abusing me over and over again under the guise of humor.

How did I stop her from continuing to do this? First, I learned to recognize it for what it actually was—abuse. Then, I tried a little humor myself. I told her I was going to try to give her a visual image of how her humor worked. I asked her to try and visualize a pigeon that flies around and releases droppings onto the shoulders of pedestrians below. By the time the person suddenly notices he or she has been messed on, the bird is long gone.

Every time after that, I was able to put the bird right back on her shoulders by commenting that I felt as though I had just been attacked by a pigeon. I identified the monster, put my cognitive defenses up, and basically said, "No, I will not accept this monster." I didn't abuse her or act defensive. I simply said that the monster wasn't mine, and I didn't deserve such treatment.

If you find yourself making insulting or snide remarks to others, or if people sometimes react to your humor with hurt or uncertainty, you might ask yourself whether you aren't in fact using humor to express anger.

Once I had pointed this out, we were able to focus on what the monster was, how it had been born, and what it meant. We had a chance to explore her history of verbal abuse along with the pain and unhappiness it had caused. The more she tapped into her own anger, the less she needed to unleash her bird of rage onto others.

If you find yourself making insulting or snide remarks to others, or if people sometimes react to your humor with hurt or uncertainty, you might ask yourself whether you aren't in fact using humor to express anger, or launching your "monster" onto their shoulders. You can start by asking yourself how you were feeling when you made the joke. Was something bothering you? Were you feeling angry? Were you feeling ashamed or guilty about something in your own life?

By exploring your own feelings you may find, to your surprise, that the joke directed at your companion really came from an inner conflict of your own, possibly stemming from abuse that you yourself had experienced. You may even recall times when you were made the butt of the same jokes you are now directing at others. In this way, you can break the cycle of verbal abuse before it can find another victim.

The Serpent:
The Monster of
Sexual Abuse

14

Don't Trust, Don't Care!

Many people who have been terribly injured by sexual abuse find it hard to develop trusting, caring relationships. If this has happened to you, then you know what a struggle it is.

I often use the image of the Serpent when talking to people about sexual abuse because the snake is the mythical creature of betrayal. From the Bible onwards the serpent has embodied a creature that seduces and destroys. Imagine a smiling serpent that leads you toward harm and you get an image of a sexual molester.

If you have been sexually abused, you may feel so hurt and betrayed that you shun relationships out of fear that you will be hurt again. You may be afraid to care about others for fear of losing the objects of your love and trust. You may use the logic that if you don't trust anyone, or don't care about anyone, you can't be hurt again. Sometimes this logic is conscious, sometimes it isn't. It may just feel as if that's "the way things are" or "standard operating procedure."

Faced with sexual trauma or abuse, many people find that turning off feelings is the fastest, most efficient way to deal with pain.

I would like to make a strong case for the importance of feeling the pain, even though that is very hard to do. Why do I say this? Because I have seen what happens when the pain is buried, bottled up, ignored, or denied.

No matter what the monster is, it is far better to uncover it and acknowledge it, painful as that may be, than to pretend it doesn't exist. Monsters don't like to be ignored. As I'll show here and in later chapters, when this happens they only grow bigger, louder, and more vicious.

> **N**o matter what the monster is, it is far better to uncover it and acknowledge it, painful as that may be, than to pretend it doesn't exist.

My work with a young man named Ken confirmed these beliefs. When I met him, Ken was 13. At the age of 4, the state had removed Ken from his home because of the sexual abuse, physical abuse, and severe neglect he experienced there.

After that, Ken lived in three different foster homes until he was adopted by his fourth foster family. Luckily, his new parents were terrific and they loved him dearly. But despite this happy turn of events, Ken still had a lot of trouble adjusting.

He had few friends, and at first his relationship with his adoptive parents was distant and cautious.

Ken was a teen at risk. Depression and the urge to commit suicide were chronic problems for him. He asked his new parents and therapist (whom Ken saw for individual treatment sessions) if he could join a psychotherapy group. Ken traveled over an hour each way to attend one of the groups that I facilitate. You'd think that if he made this kind of effort, he'd be champing at the bit to contribute, right?

Far from it. When Ken would get to group, he'd say absolutely nothing. His silence lasted through the entire session. It was clear that he was anxious, but when his peers asked him why he was so quiet Ken said he had nothing to say. He would loyally and at great effort show up every week, just to say nothing!

Finally, feeling quite concerned, I and the other group members started probing a bit more deeply. We asked Ken what his feelings were for the group as a whole and for particular group members. He said nobody mattered to him at all.

We asked Ken to tell us which meant more to him, the tip of his fingernail or the people in the room. He couldn't respond.

We asked Ken if he trusted anyone in the room. Again he refused to say a word.

What we were seeing right before our eyes was his basic problem: he couldn't trust or show that he cared about people. The trauma he had experienced in childhood, the abuse that was then followed by the loss of his parental ties, were being played out every single day of his life, in every relationship in his life. It was as if he had a monster on his shoulder that kept whispering into his ear, "Don't trust! Don't care!" It was really very sad to see just how much damage had been done to this boy.

There were, however, two things working in Ken's favor. One was a growing track record of good feelings and attachment to his adoptive parents. The second was Ken's innate ability to feel loyal to people who were good to him (some kids who have been abused lose even this ability). So although Ken couldn't acknowledge trust and concern, he could maintain some kind of relationship. These two facts allowed him to continue the work in therapy.

It was not easy for Ken to learn how to deal with his horrible monster. He had to fight a great battle to win back his mind and soul. The monster was interfering with his ability to open up and express his appreciation and affection for people. Eventually, his internal pain grew too great, and he needed to be hospitalized. On the positive side, this allowed us to do intensive psychotherapy without having to worry too much about self-destructive behavior or attempted suicide.

The therapy took the form of methods I'll address later in discussing how you set goals and move toward healing. Basically, though, we performed a "monsterectomy." We used writing therapy, followed by gradual, slow steps where Ken shared the secrets of his painful past. Ken had never before been able to tell anyone the details of what had happened to him. The sexual abuse had been too horrible.

Not only was Ken ultimately able to share the past with me and with his friends his own age in the hospital, but he also took a giant step towards moving beyond the abuse by sharing his story with his adoptive parents and sister. Ken was pleased to witness his new family's outrage because it meant they cared for him, loved him, and wanted to protect him. Finally, in a very real sense, Ken was able to "come home."

For the first time in his life, Ken felt he had moved through some of the barriers in his relationships. The past abuse had taught him not to trust, but after sharing his secrets he saw that some people, like the loving family now putting their arms around him, could be trusted. The abuse had taught him not to care, but after facing his monsters, he gained power over them and they no longer stood between him and other people. He no longer had to experience isolation and numbness. Through his own agonizingly hard work, this young man was able to begin re-making his life and his very being.

Today Ken is working to sustain the true intimacy and warmth he achieved. Though there have been ups and downs along the road, he is supported by people who love him very much and want nothing more than for him to be happy. He would never have reached this point had he not let himself trust and care.

I will never forget Ken, I think, because of his great courage and fierce determination to fight the awful abuse inflicted on him, and also because of what he taught me about the power of love.

If, as you read this, you see yourself in Ken, know that there is hope beyond the pain.

The monsters born of abuse and trauma are powerful. They can destroy a life. But by finding them, talking to them, learning as much as you can about them, and then refusing to let them defeat you, you CAN free yourself. This book is here to help you do that.

15

The V Word

I'd like to share with you another story that demonstrates that, no matter what happens to you along life's rough road, no matter what mythical monsters you may be struggling with, you CAN succeed.

A valiant young person who has learned to name and conquer her monsters is a teenage girl named Katy. It is a sad truth that sexual development, as natural a process as rain falling from the sky, or peaches ripening on the vine, can become a traumatic event when abuse is part of the picture. This is complicated even further when a person is influenced by our society's unspoken taboo against sexual pleasure.

Katy was 15 years old and a virgin. Like so many others, she had a traumatic past. The youngest of eight children, Katy had received little attention from her mother and stepfather who were preoccupied with their demanding careers. Katy's biological father, a driven workaholic, had sexually abused her and then abandoned her emotionally. As she grew into her teenage years, Katy began to have difficulty dealing with relationships, especially relationships with the opposite sex.

Finally, though, she thought she had met someone who could understand and have the kind of patience that she needed. She opened her heart to him and decided to trust him. And with her trust went her virginity.

A week after her losing "the V word" (as Katy called it in extreme embarrassment), the young man dumped her. Katy was devastated. Probably the most painful thing to her was that she had dreamed of giving her virginity to someone special. She didn't realize that he would turn out to be something less than expected. Her friends had always told her, "Make sure you lose it with someone really great." Katy found herself thinking about how stupid and naive she was. She was "distraught with humiliation," she said. She talked about suicide, and I almost hospitalized her.

The more we talked, the more it became clear that she was carrying a monster on her shoulder that liked to make speeches. Katy's monster said to her, "You must be perfect; you must bat a thousand. Anything less than perfect means that you're a failure. You can't make a mistake when it comes to sex, even if it is your first time, especially if it is your first time!"

In light of her too early and painful introduction to sexual matters, it was natural that Katy hoped for a positive sexual experience the way she imagined it was supposed to be. Since most victims of sexual abuse feel that it was somehow their fault, it's possible that Katy had wanted this new experience to somehow cancel out the pain and guilt she felt from the earlier abusive one. The unvarnished reality that first-time sex may not meet a standard of perfection—it may hurt, it may take time to feel relaxed, and so forth—didn't enter into Katy's fantasy. And so she felt double the pain, turning a simple mistake in judgment (picking the wrong guy) into a tragedy and terrible disappointment.

Katy had trouble moving on with her life because of the monster of abuse or serpent constantly hissing into her ear, reminders of how awful she was. Words like "slut," "reject," "cheap," and "tramp" echoed in her head. The monster was punishing her for being less than perfect, for being human, and for trying to enjoy sex. Abuse from her past had taught her sex was dirty, sex was shameful. Katy had expected to wipe out the memory of that bad experience from her past by entering into a loving one with this man. When it failed miserably, she felt stupid, full of confusing feelings, and certain that this mistake was unforgivable.

How did Katy help herself? First, she wrote a letter to the man who rejected her, expressing her pain. As she wrote, her anger poured out. So severely had she been hurt by her abusive father that she was poorly equipped to handle the awkward blunders of a first relationship and losing her virginity as well.

> So severely had she been hurt by her abusive father that she was poorly equipped to handle the awkward blunders of a first relationship.

Katy realized that because of her guilt about sexuality, she had taken on her father's monster of abuse and made it her own. The writing and talking therapy helped her identify the monster's rightful owner. As she explored her feelings about sex and the abuse from her past, she was able to gain a clearer picture of herself and her natural desires. She eventually freed herself from two very powerful monsters: the idea that losing one's virginity has to be a wonderful experience; and the legacy of her abuse which told her that sexuality is bad and leads to rejection and abandonment. Like Ken, Katy is a victor.

16

All I'm Good for is Sex

As I showed in the example of "the battered brother" in Chapter 4, one of the most painful aspects of abuse is that the pain is bound up with the love.

"Identification with the aggressor" is a phrase psychologists use to describe a cluster of feelings having to do with a victim's connection to the abuser. By cementing pain with pleasure, abuse creates a kind of myth within the mind of the victim, that love is experienced as pain.

Giving up the abuse may mean giving up someone who is loved or cherished in other ways.

Giving up the abuse may mean giving up someone who is loved or cherished in other ways. This is very hard to do. In a strange way, the mind can find it preferable to identify with the abuser and see his beliefs, problems, or standards as one's own. This is true not only of childhood sexual abuse but also of sexual abuse experienced as an adolescent or young adult.

Let's take the example of date rape, or acquaintance rape. Although there are exceptions, girls from abusive homes can be especially vulnerable to this kind of experience. In a way, it can seem the confirmation of the distorted image they hold of themselves as a result of their childhood abuse. One of the awful lessons children learn from sexual abuse is that their very humanity means nothing; their feelings mean nothing; their privacy means nothing.

The abuser's monster says to the victim, "All you're good for is sex." The child then grows up believing this about herself. The long arms of this serpent-monster can stretch far into adulthood, damaging a woman's sense of her own self-worth and destroying her ability to love and to work.

When date rape occurs, it confirms this monstrous message or "myth" that the woman has adopted for herself. A young woman I worked with showed this myth in action. Linda was a bright and active high school senior who had a lot going for her, but she had also suffered sexual abuse at the hands of her father. She was insecure when it came to trusting men. Her insecurity intensified when a young man she knew forced himself on her after a school dance.

Linda felt devastated. She had known this fellow since childhood and couldn't believe that he

71

would betray her in this way. She felt she had been naive to trust him, and that the event was her fault. Furthermore, she found it humiliating to have to see him day after day on the streets of their small town. This seems to be typical of many victims of date rape. Many young women like Linda continue to see their abusers at parties, in classes, or when walking home from school. They may socialize with the same group of friends or hang out at the same places.

Each time Linda saw the rapist her pain increased. She found herself struggling for some sense of self-control. She tried confronting the young man and imposing limits on him, rather than just ignoring him, but every time she confronted him, he'd find a way of getting through to her, by "stealing" a kiss or taking one of her possessions. Without meaning to, Linda was setting herself up for repeated abuse. Because of her low self-esteem and the monster on her shoulder that told her she was just good for sex, not love, Linda unwisely was seeking some relief from the very person who had harmed her.

One day, Linda again confronted the young man, and this time it was she who demanded sex. From her point of view, she had taken back control by treating him the same way he had treated her. In a sense, she was trying to put the monster back on his shoulders where it belonged. She didn't feel exploited. In fact, afterward she felt even greater self-confidence.

When we talked about it, though, Linda realized that what she had done was to accept her perpetrator's values. In a sense, she had found her emotional relief by becoming the sexual aggressor herself. She played by his rules and confirmed his definition of who she was (a sexual object). His rules included the idea that personal power comes through sexual control. As we talked, Linda saw that it wasn't sex she'd been engaged in but a power struggle.

Linda's experience shows that when you harbor a monster of shame and guilt, it is sometimes easier to adopt the values of your abuser than to separate from him. For Linda, it was less painful to behave like her abuser than it was to lose him and feel that pain directly. It is important to understand all the confusing feelings and issues that come from abuse.

The bottom line: It is far better to stare down your own monsters than to adopt those of someone who uses or hurts you.

17

If You Love Me, it Wasn't Rape

Some women respond to the trauma of rape by taking the stance that if the rapist could only love them, it would be as if the rape never happened.

Even if a young woman was not the victim of childhood abuse as Linda was in the previous chapter, rape still leaves a terrible monster of shame and guilt on the shoulder of the victim, and it's hard work to remove it. Again, there can be a complex connection between the abuser and the survivor.

A victim's feelings after an acquaintance rape can be very confusing. One 14-year-old girl told me that after she had been raped by a friend, he told her that he loved her. Her reaction was, "I told myself that it couldn't be rape if he loved me."

A 16-year-old was raped by a young man she partied with one evening on an ocean cruise. The next morning she saw him with two girls "fawning all over him." Her first reaction was jealousy.

Imagine feeling jealous that another woman has the attention of a man who raped you! In Monster Therapy terms, it is like wanting to gain the love of a monster or horrible snake that has just bitten you.

A young woman I worked with who had been repeatedly raped by an acquaintance told me that she had a recurring fantasy. She confided in me that the best thing that could happen to her would be for the fellow to tell her he loved her. "Then we could get married, have children, live happily ever after, and I could quit therapy."

The thinking in these cases seems to go something like this: "I can be free of the symptoms of rape if what happened wasn't really rape. Maybe it's his way of getting close to me. Maybe he doesn't have very good communication skills and is kind of rough with sex – a 'man' thing. So, if it wasn't really rape, I shouldn't feel so upset."

Nobody wants to believe they were raped and more than that, suffer the painful shame that goes with it. You go back hoping you were wrong and he will be nice. If he would just apologize, acknowledge your hurt feelings and give you some affection, then what happened wouldn't have to be seen as rape. It's as though the one who causes the pain also has the power to take it away.

The problem with this type of thinking is that it keeps the abuser in the driver's seat. By seeking comfort from your abuser, you give him or her enormous control. It makes you dependent on his approval and caring. This can increase your feelings of shame because, on some level, this powerlessness feels wrong. Even more tragic is that, by continuing to be involved with him this way, you could be in physical danger again as well.

I have met women who have gone back to their abusers out of fear; but others have gone back because this was the only person who gave them any "affection." This often occurs with younger girls whose parents are relatively uninvolved with them.

If you have this monster on your shoulder, the one that says, "It wasn't rape. Rape can't happen to me," then a first step will be to face your own denial. Then, hard though it may be, you can explore how the abuse has affected the way you think and feel about yourself. When you have identified the monster of shame and guilt on your shoulder and really sketched it fully in your mind, you will be on the road to reclaiming the self-esteem you lost as a result of the abuse.

The Chameleon:
The Monster of Rejection

18

Racism is Abuse, Too

There is another kind of abuse that can be painful and damaging, and that is the abuse that comes from cultural rejection. Society's demand that you be or act differently from what you are inside can be terribly painful. It can make you feel that there is no place for you, that the "real you" cannot be loved or accepted.

I like to use the image of the Chameleon for this cultural monster because it captures the essence of society's message: change yourself, be something that you are not. The chameleon is legendary for being able to change its color and appearance at will, and it symbolizes a creature that can adapt to anything. But adapting is not necessarily the highest good for a human being. Being yourself is.

As a child and adolescent psychiatrist, I have had the unique opportunity to see the way racism affects children as they are growing up. Even though the kids I see are troubled, they do reflect the larger social trends. In fact, they're more sensitive to these trends precisely because they are vulnerable.

You might think that minority youth today are savvy to the effects of racism, but I've found that many minority youths can be easily fooled by blatant racism and actually do things to let the racists off the hook. It's a kind of denial similar to the rape victim's willingness to see the rapist as loving and kind. That is why I always ask minority youths about the potential effects of racism on their lives.

I've found that many minority youths can be easily fooled by blatant racism and actually do things to let the racists off the hook.

A few years ago I worked with an African-American teenager who had severe behavioral problems. Teachers and peers had labeled Martin as a "bad" kid. Martin denied he was ever a victim of racism. But when we talked I learned that his so-called "friends" often called him "nigger." He thought it was cool that they called him that because they were his friends. He liked the way the word itself seemed to make everyone more comfortable with each other.

As Martin developed a keener sense of what racism looks and feels like again, naming the monster, he realized that racism is itself a monster. In Martin's case, the monster sat on his shoulder telling him that he had no right to complain, that he was good for nothing, and that he deserved to be called by an insulting name.

Martin also related a story that showed he was becoming aware of how his own acting out played a part in this complex process. Martin had gone to a friend's party, but as soon as he got there he was quickly asked to leave. When he asked his friend why, the friend said it was his parents' wish. Martin was naturally very upset. On his way out, he intentionally broke a vase and shattered the glass storm door.

Did racism play a role in Martin's unacceptable acting out? Martin firmly denied it. He said that his friends' parents had thrown him out because he was "bad." But the "bad" behavior had occurred as he was leaving, after he had already been rejected. It eventually became clear that Martin broke the glass because he wanted to be rejected for his behavior, not for the color of his skin. So racism was indeed playing a role. The more we talked, the more Martin described how unbearable it was to be rejected for your race. But your behavior? That's not so bad. And being rejected for your behavior allows you to remain friends with the very people who are a part of the racist process.

I have seen minority youths suffer from other monsters of racism. For example, I have worked with African-American youths who believe the only way they can possibly attend college is through an athletic scholarship. They see themselves as inherently unworthy of a college scholarship unless they get it for athletic achievement. See the monster? It's saying to these kids that they are only good as athletic machines. This is demeaning, and it can lead to minority kids giving up their pursuit of learning if they find that for some reason they can't participate in sports.

Racism, like all prejudice, is a monster that says, "Anyone different from me is dangerous, is bad." To achieve their full potential, victims of racism need to identify these vicious monsters and reject them.

19

Be a Real Woman

Along with racism, sexism is another hurtful monster that says to men and women, "You are not okay just as you are." Sexism is a kind of ongoing abuse that strips people of their sense of innate value.

Women and men each struggle in their own ways with this killer monster. For many women, the problem seems especially painful. Often these

> **S**exism is a kind of ongoing abuse that strips people of their sense of innate value. Women and men each struggle in their own ways with this killer monster.

women have very low self-esteem, and they derive their sense of self-worth from living up to certain men's expectations. They seem to accept the rules and expectations of the "male chauvinist pig" mentality. The female "male chauvinist pig" unwittingly turns the male sexist monster on herself.

The monster on the shoulder of these women focuses on their physical appearance. How many women are starving themselves, dieting and working out day after grueling day? Admittedly there are many women who do this just for themselves and their own sense of femininity and health. However there are countless others who are struggling to look more "beautiful and sexy" according to a narrow view circumscribed by the male chauvinist. This is terribly demeaning. It encourages women to desire to be what they are not, damage their bodies in the process, defy common sense and good health, and then wait around for men to notice so they can use them as sexual objects. This cultural norm should be seen for what it is: a sexist monster!

I often see this monster on the shoulders of women with eating disorders. Many of the young women I see in treatment have a rigid sense of what it means to be attractive. They think they are trying very hard to live up to their own standards of beauty, while in fact, they are trying to live up to the monster inside that whispers to them that their bodies are not alright just as nature made them. They crave an impossible ideal because the monster says that this will bring friends, admiration, and love.

Alice, a young woman with anorexia, had to work very hard in treatment to overcome these unrealistic ideals. Our sessions focused on rebuilding her self-esteem. Alice had many wonderful qualities; she was friendly, smart, and brave, but she felt these meant nothing if she couldn't, in her words, "look like Brooke Shields."

Alice had a history of sexual abuse, which is common among women with eating disorders. She had learned to see herself only as a sexual object, one whose sole value was as a pretty bauble or toy. If she couldn't be a movie star, then in her mind, she had no worth. That's what abuse had taught her. Beauty is only part of the picture, but the sexist monster says "That's all there is."

Treatment involves unraveling this falsehood. We worked on restoring Alice's ability to value other parts of herself, and to see herself as a full person with a range of talents and assets. I also worked with Alice's parents, who were unknowingly promoting this sexist image through their own preoccupation with looks, image, and glamour.

Men, too, have their own struggles with the sexist monster and the myth of what they should be. For many men, the sexist monster usually focuses on other issues besides looks, usually, power, money, and a narrowly defined view of success. Some men may place too much emphasis on "having" a woman who is "gorgeous" in order to make them feel "more like a man." All of these assumptions need to be challenged and changed. They are just more of society's little sexist monsters on our shoulders.

But in general, men seem to be in greater control and to suffer less humiliation from sexist beliefs. Thus, men can be especially helpful in changing sexist attitudes and the cycle of abuse that is damaging the health of so many women. As fathers, men can play a unique role in teaching new generations of women about their own innate value. Instead of supporting sexist beliefs through demeaning comments or actions, fathers can teach their daughters how valuable they are as well-rounded human beings. They can also teach their sons how to respect and appreciate the nonsexual qualities in women.

If we all pull together, we may be able to change the face of the sexist monster to a kind, loving creature that accepts and loves all people, not for what they look like, but for who they are inside.

20

Be a Real Man

Perhaps nothing is as private and vulnerable as our sexual identity. At the core of our identities is a sense of ourselves as sexual beings. Perhaps this is why issues around homosexuality provoke such outrage, anger, denial, fear, and pain. Something about this complex set of feelings engages our deepest emotions.

As a culture, we are intolerant of homosexuality. The myth of homosexuality is that it is something that a person should change in order to fit in better with society.

> The myth of homosexuality is that it is something that a person should change in order to fit in better with society.

I once worked with a 50-year-old homosexual man who came into treatment for depression. Roger was a mature man with grown children. He reported that he had been happily married until his wife's unexpected death years earlier. He spoke of feeling very happy with his homosexuality and had no desire to change that aspect of his life. He had many other issues he wished to address, however, many other feelings he wanted to understand.

As his therapy progressed, it came out that he had been sexually abused as a child. Roger's father had sexually molested him when he was 17 years old. He could not remember any other abuse by his father and he never found out if his father was a practicing homosexual. But he did recall abuse by others.

Between the ages of six and ten, he was abused by a teacher at school. Then at age 13, he was forced to have sex with a monk in his church. Roger's father was away from home a great deal, travelling on business, and Roger craved attention from an older man. He felt lonely and found these sexual relationships nurturing and comforting. He had no idea then that he was being abused by the adults around him.

To deal with the monster of abuse, Roger worked through his past much the way Ken and Katy did. He came to recognize that, as a child, he had been vulnerable to these adults. They had taken advantage of his childish needs for love and attention. Now, on top of that, Roger had to begin another long process of dealing with society's monster: disapproval of his gay lifestyle.

A tragedy continues to be that many homosexuals spend time, money, and emotional energy trying to fit in. This means trying to be heterosexual. Many gay people get married, have children, and hope that somehow their feelings will change.

For Roger, treatment became an exploration of why he felt he had "to fit in." We discussed at length each of the theories of homosexuality. As Roger explored the origins of his feelings, he realized that he really wasn't interested in changing his orientation. It became obvious that "Why am I gay?" was a monster on his shoulder. It was not his own question but instead was the question of a monster he had created from society's condemnation of him, from the myth of the "real" man. When he realized that the monster was not really his, but society's, he was able to shrug off the sense of shame and guilt and get on with his life, and his depression lifted.

Roger's life is a good example of monsters in action and how sometimes we take on monsters that are not our own.

Part 3
Steps to Recovery

21

Courage and Recovery

Open letter to all Survivors of Abuse:

If you are reading this and have been a victim of abuse, you should know that, contrary to what most victims believe about themselves—that they are flawed, guilty, or even dirty—you are, in fact, brave and courageous. Rising up from despair and dealing with painful memories and feelings are acts of courage. You are examples of the very bravest that exist in human beings.

Time and again I have witnessed in survivors a tenacious desire to recover from the pain they have experienced. I have had the opportunity and privilege to watch and assist many people through this recovery process. I have always been amazed at what the human spirit is capable of accomplishing under such difficult circumstances.

If you are in recovery, or even if you are just at the beginning of your journey to understanding, you are very brave. Hold this truth in your heart through the long and difficult soul-searching that lies ahead.

People like you are survivors of childhood abuse, physical and emotional abuse, neglect, or sexual assault. It is important for you to understand that the monster jumps onto your shoulder during the abusive act. You may not have been able to refuse the abuse when it occurred, but you can learn to refuse the guilt, shame, and responsibility for what happened. It is possible to learn how to kick these monsters off your shoulders and get on with your life.

Y ou may not have been able to refuse the abuse when it occurred, but you can learn to refuse the guilt, shame, and responsibility for what happened.

I hope that from what you have read so far, you are developing a clearer image of what the "monster" of abuse is and how it can affect your life. The next step is learning to free yourself from the monster and taking back control of yourself. Remember, be patient. Recovery does not happen overnight. Be patient with setbacks when they come and forgive yourself for not being perfect. Your courage and hard work will be rewarded with a better understanding of yourself and in-creased self-respect and self-love.

Respectfully yours,
David J. Schopick, M.D.

Now that you know where you're headed in this process toward self-love and self-respect, you can work on identifying manageable steps to get there. That's what Parts 3 and 4 of this book are designed to help you do. In the following chapters, you will learn how to identify methods you can use to help you separate from the abuse. You can learn to change the way you think, feel, and communicate so that you are no longer victimized in relationships.

> You can learn to change the way you think, feel, and communicate so that you are no longer victimized in relationships.

Part 3 covers different aspects of the recovery process, while focusing on psychotherapy as the foundation for healing. There are many types of therapeutic settings available. Individual psycho-therapy, where you are one-on-one with a trained therapist, psychiatrist, or social worker, is perhaps the most intense and, certainly, the most private.

Group therapy is where you share experiences and support with a group that has a trained thera-pist leading it. When you can tell your story looking into the eyes of your peers, and see respect and validation there, then you will have taken a major step in your recovery.

Sometimes family therapy is best, so you can talk about painful feelings directly with other family members.

Part 4 provides specific exercises you can use whether you are in psychotherapy or not. These include writing therapy, art therapy, self-hypnosis, and visualization techniques. Teaching you how to take control of your thoughts and feelings is the goal. We want you, not your monster, to be in control.

22

Confronting the Perpetrator

In the ideal world, survivors of abuse would have the opportunity to confront the perpetrator. They would do so without having to back down from the confrontation.

However, in reality it doesn't work this way. It is important to recognize that the goal of recovery is not an apology from the perpetrator. Seeking an apology places you, once again, within the perpetrator's power or control. The goal of therapy

> The goal of recovery is not an apology from the perpetrator. Seeking an apology places you, once again, within the perpetrator's power or control.

here is to put you, the survivor, in control of your thoughts and feelings. The reward is increased personal power, self-love, and self-respect. You do not need another person to do this.

Monster Therapy is about learning to identify ways of healing successfully on your own. It is about re-making the myths inside your own mind, giving YOU the power and control, not about seeking it from somebody else to grant to you. Needing a particular response such as a confession or apology is a set-up for a control struggle and, in some cases, could place you in physical danger. Furthermore, looking for a response from another person interferes with your recovery by shifting the focus away from yourself, your own monsters, and the work you need to do.

Whenever one of my patients expresses a wish to confront the perpetrator, I try to find out what that person hopes to gain from the encounter. If the goal is an apology, I try to persuade them that they are setting themselves up for failure. Even if the perpetrator would do all the "right" things, I still would not encourage such a meeting because it feeds into the control that the perpetrator enjoys. Since it also fosters the victim's fear and sense of powerlessness, there is a risk of revictimization.

It can also be dangerous for adults to express their feelings of anger or disappointment. For example, women who are victims of rape or spousal abuse may provoke a brutal response if they voice their pain and outrage directly to their abuser.

There are many other reasons confrontation with the perpetrator may be unwise or even impossible. He or she may be dead, may have moved away, or simply be unwilling to participate. In other cases, it's impractical to seek a response. In cases of cultural abuse—racism, sexism, or homophobia—it would be impossible to gain an apology from an entire society. In some cases, the abuse itself makes victims feel so powerless that confronting their perpetrators is the last thing they can imagine doing.

Sometimes victims of abuse decide to criminally prosecute their abusers. As a psychiatrist concerned with my patient's recovery, I would never make such a recommendation without knowing the details of a person's situation. Although criminal prosecution can be an empowering step, it is stressful, and can actually make symptoms worse. There will be interviews by the police and prosecuting attorneys. Court appearances during a trial can be frightening and there could be grand jury appearances. The legal process can drag on endlessly, adding to the victim's distress and the abuser may seek revenge. The victim has no control over police officers, prosecutors, or jurors and the victim's efforts may not be rewarded with a conviction.

I encourage my patients who do seek legal redress to make sure they have adequate support systems in place before embarking on this stressful course. I do think it is reasonable and positive to seek legal prosecution, but I believe the ultimate victory must occur within the victim's mind and heart. I urge persons who take this course to consider success as the act of standing up and insisting that justice be done. Then, no matter what the outcome, they "win."

There is nothing wrong with expressing your outrage and pain. In fact, it is absolutely necessary that you do, as I'll explain in the chapters that follow. But the person to voice it to is yourself, not the abuser. The best way to separate yourself from the abuse and take back your own power is to recognize which monsters are yours and which belong to the abuser. By focusing on what you can change in your inner world, and through that, your relationships with other people, you can gradually rebuild your self-esteem. You will be able to move on with your life without the extreme anger, guilt, shame, and powerlessness that may have crippled you in the past.

Freeing yourself from "the monsters on your shoulder" comes from understanding yourself better, how your mind works, and what kinds of monsters linger within your psyche. This is the essential task, whether you choose to do it on your own, through individual therapy, group therapy, family therapy, or other healing techniques.

23

Learning to Trust

Abuse has a remarkable way of interfering with a person's ability to trust. One of the first steps on the road to recovery is learning how to trust again.

You may remember the story of Ken in Part 2, whose inner monster kept telling him, "Don't trust, don't care!" This is a common legacy of abuse. Notice that as part of Ken's recovery, trusting came before caring. Trust always precedes other positive feelings; it is the bedrock on which a relationship is built.

Often, people will go to the trouble of finding a therapist, arrange their schedules to show up on time, juggle their budget to pay for the session, and then when they get there, gloss over the troubling subjects of their lives or even sometimes refuse to talk altogether.

Abuse is so damaging it can even interfere with the trust that is required when a person is trying to change. Often, people will go to the trouble of finding a therapist, arrange their schedules to show up on time, juggle their budget to pay for the session, and then when they get there, gloss over the troubling subjects of their lives or even sometimes refuse to talk altogether.

The situation is not unlike one in which a person is swimming in a river with a dangerous waterfall just downstream. The terrified swimmer screams for help. Luckily, someone on shore hears the cries and runs to the river's edge to assist with a rescue. The rescuer holds out his hand; the swimmer struggles closer to the shore. But just when they're within arm's reach of each other, unbelievably, the swimmer turns away from the rescuer's outstretched hand. The swimmer is pulled by the river's current toward an uncertain destiny.

Terribly confused by this kind of behavior, I began to ask people why they were doing it. The answers I got were very simple: some said they were afraid that when they extended their hands to the rescuer, the rescuer would pull his hand away or worse yet, they'd get clubbed over the head by the so-called "rescuer." Others said they were used to going over waterfalls; that's how they experienced life, one whitewater wave after another. To others, grabbing on to a helping hand was even more terrifying than rushing toward the watery abyss. They'd rather take their chances with the river than risk trusting and getting burned.

In my experience, people who have been abused suffer this fear of trust because of the betrayal and feelings of isolation they experienced earlier in their lives. This is especially true for persons who have been sexually abused. Often the perpetrator taught them how not to trust by teaching them to keep secrets. Not surprisingly, keeping secrets is a hallmark of the dysfunctional or abusive home. Pedophiles often build a child's "trust" in them by sharing little confidences with them. Then they ask the child to promise not to tell his or her parents about "our" secret. Sometimes it starts with little things, innocent violations of the parents' rules, like watching a forbidden TV show, or staying up past bedtime. Then it can escalate to watching a pornographic video together, or "harmless" touches. Finally there comes a point at which the abuser takes full advantage of the child. By this time, the child will not tell the parents what's going on because the child has been seduced into keeping secrets. Once the sex actually happens, the child often feels terribly isolated from the parents, emotionally cut off from them. As a result, in addition to the sexual violation that has just taken place, the child's sense of trust with his or her own parents has also been violated.

This principle, the connection between abuse and keeping secrets, can be turned to your advantage now that you are in the process of recovery. You can learn to recognize secrets as a kind of "monster danger signal." If someone in your present life tells or asks you to keep a secret, look out. Usually keeping a secret requires that you create a barrier between yourself and somebody else, often someone whom you trust and love. When the barriers go up, trust diminishes.

Keeping secrets can also apply to the voices of your own "inner monsters." Monsters love secrets. They love walls, caves, and dark places. They want to hide and not be brought into the light. You may find yourself thinking things like, "I can't tell my therapist (family, friends) about THAT. I could never talk about THAT." That's the monster of shame and guilt talking.

> **K**eeping secrets is a hallmark of the dys-functional or abusive home.

While it's certainly true that there can be experiences so private you won't want to share them with most people in your life, it's also true that keeping secrets from those who have earned the right to be trusted such as a concerned friend, loving family member, or therapist who is trying to help you only reinforces the walls of distrust built by your abuser.

When you are first learning to trust, it's wise to take time to get to know someone, to see a track record of good actions, before bestowing your trust in them. In fact, the person who demands that you instantly "trust me" before you can see evidence of his or her trustworthiness, probably should not be trusted.

It's a cliché, but nevertheless true, that a good rule of thumb is "actions speak louder than words." The phrase "trust me" is hollow without the deeds to back it up.

However, when someone has earned your trust through their right actions, when they have shown their willingness to meet you halfway, to give as much as they take, and to treat you with respect, then it is up to you to decide whether to take the risk and hold out your hand or "hang back with the monster" that says "Don't trust, don't care!" The choice is yours.

24

Psychotherapy and the Monster

If keeping secrets is the hallmark of a dysfunctional or abusive home, then sharing secrets, opening all the locked doors, letting all the monsters out of the darkness, is the hallmark of psychotherapy.

If keeping secrets is the hallmark of a dysfunctional or abusive home, then sharing secrets, opening all the locked doors, letting all the monsters out of the darkness, is the hallmark of psychotherapy.

There are many ways to think about psychotherapy and the process of recovery. Therapists, researchers, and people in treatment have many different theories about how the healing actually takes place.

I believe that the sharing of secret monsters is a key way in which therapy helps to transform a person. It's as if the tremendous relief of just voicing all the "monster talk" has a therapeutic effect.

When Dante wrote his classic poem, *The Inferno*, about climbing up out of hell, he envisioned hell as a place over which there was a sign that read: "Abandon all hope, ye who enter here."

Sometimes I feel as if over a therapist's office there should be a sign that reads: "Abandon all secrets, ye who enter here."

Secrets are the way your inner self keeps you weighed down with all those huge monsters that you've lived with for so long. Secrets are like your

> **S**ecrets are the way your inner self keeps you weighed down with all those huge monsters that you've lived with for so long.

monster's blackmail. Every time you recall the abuse, your inner monster punishes you. It urges you not to tell anyone about what happened: "If people ever find out, they'll hate you!" says the monster. "They'll see you as damaged!"

For you to become well again, the secrets must come out. The reality is, the shame and guilt are not yours; they do not belong to you. They belong to the abuser.

During psychotherapy, all the secrets and all the secret monsters can come out, be closely examined, and be healed. It's where you can sort out all the shame, guilt, and terror that may have plagued you since the abuse.

Therapy works through the process of "transference." This means you transfer feelings and attitudes toward people in your past onto people in the present, especially onto the therapist. You then have the chance to examine them in a neutral way to try to understand what they mean and how they may be affecting you.

For you to become well again, the secrets must come out.

In other words, therapy is a safe place where you can experience emotion. This may sound simplistic, but it's true. Many abuse victims say they have never felt safe anywhere, because of what happened to them. For abuse victims, the therapist's office is a place where they can feel safe, maybe for the first time in their lives.

Experiencing emotion is essential to restructuring your view of yourself. In our culture, emotional release is generally viewed as a sign of weakness. In therapy, however, we learn that releasing anger, rage, grief, pain, loss, and fear, as well as joy and pleasure, are necessary steps toward self-knowledge and growth.

In Monster Therapy terms, we might describe the purpose of therapy as one in which you become the master, instead of the monster being the master. In a way, it means releasing the "monster" inside you so you can look at it, describe it, name it, and finally move beyond it.

The goal of treatment is to learn new ways to relate to yourself and to others. An important step in this goal is learning to communicate your needs, feelings, wishes, and fears more effectively. In therapy, anger is not acted out but instead is expressed, understood, and worked through.

In Monster Therapy terms, we might describe the purpose of therapy as one in which you become the master, instead of the monster being the master.

Because of the feelings and issues raised in treatment, trust is a vital part of the relationship. You don't necessarily have to trust the therapist right away, but trust should grow over time. If this does not happen in treatment, it may mean that something is wrong in the basic pact between you and your therapist. These concerns should also be talked about and dealt with. (See Chapters 28 and 29 on therapists and their monsters.)

However, even when there is a basic level of trust, there still may be times when you become quite angry at the therapist. Sometimes it may seem as though you are dumping your anger onto the therapist. This may be a result of transference, since this process involves not only transferring warm and loving feelings but also negative and hostile feelings. It's important not to reduce or negate your feelings by dismissing them as "just transference." The task in treatment is to understand the source of the feelings and how they affect you.

If your therapist is one who says very little during the session, this transference can become stronger. The silence becomes like a vacuum that you will fill with memories and associations from past relationships. If this occurs, you have some choices. If your therapist's silence bothers you, I suggest that you discuss your feelings directly with the therapist. You can explain that the relative silence makes you very anxious. You may want to probe beneath the surface to explore where the fear comes from. Most people avoid these kinds of amiable or neutral confrontations because they cause stress. But just discussing this problem within the therapy can be very therapeutic. If you can't do it with your therapist, a person committed to your well-being, then how will you learn to do it with others?

In treatment, you and the therapist are there to work together on discovering new ways to interact that are comfortable for you and others. Why waste a wonderful opportunity to learn about yourself and perhaps develop new goals for personal change?

A word about a therapist's style. We all have our quirks. But that doesn't prevent us from being good therapists. In fact, it can help you and your therapist if you both are willing to discuss how your styles and personalities affect each other. That good communication can promote your recovery. The goal is to bring everything, all the monsters, all the feelings and experiences, into the light. The chapters on communication techniques can help you speak more directly about your feelings, both loving and angry.

Hiding your feelings during treatment will only undermine the therapy. Hiding your feelings is like keeping secrets, something you may have learned to do when you were growing up. These secrets can poison a relationship. They seem to feed the monsters in all of us by arousing our feelings of suspicion, fear, and aloneness. So please, to the extent that you are able, try to bring all of yourself and your concerns into the therapy.

Building a new life means building a new foundation of trust and communication. It means taking the monster off your shoulder, putting it "on the table" between you and your therapist, and saying, "What have we got here?"

And that's when the healing begins.

25

A New Family Order

Including your family in the recovery process can be a powerful step in therapy.

In the same way that individuals carry monsters on their shoulders, a family unit can have group monsters on their shoulders. Looking at these mythic monsters can be central to family therapy. In fact, much of a family's therapeutic work involves rewriting or retelling family stories. This includes beliefs about the family as a whole and about individual family members.

Family therapy is an opportunity for family members to reject the old rules of deception and establish new ones of trust and honesty. Exposing secrets within the family during therapy sessions can powerfully transform these relationships to healthier levels.

As a psychiatrist, I look for allies in the treatment process wherever I can find them. The family (or some members of the family) can be an excellent resource. This is especially true when siblings are close and can support each other.

It is best if you, too, can view your family as a resource for renewal, as a creative wellspring for new myths rather than a beast of burden. Unfortunately, in families where abuse has occurred, family members may feel alienated and angry toward each other. However, this very tension can make family therapy a welcome vehicle for change, for learning to develop new relationships of trust and sharing.

The process usually requires stamina and persistence while painful secrets are uncovered. Some members of the family reveal how they were abused, either mentally, physically, or sexually. Other family members may have no knowledge of someone else being abused. They may only be aware of their own abuse and emotional torture.

For example, I worked with a young woman who was jealous of her father's apparent preference for an older sister. What she didn't realize was that the older sister was allowing herself to be sexually abused in order to keep their father from molesting her younger sister! As is all too common, the father was clearly abusing one and inadvertently abusing the other without either girl's knowledge.

Another aspect of family therapy you may find upsetting is the urge to direct your anger toward the non-abusive parent for failing to protect you. At the same time, you may also feel protective of this parent by rationalizing what happened: "Mom didn't feel she could support us on her own." "Mom had no idea what was going on." "What good will it do to get angry at her? She didn't have anything to do with it."

Whether you like it or not, however, there usually exists enormous anger toward the non-abusive parent. In order to heal the family and foster honesty among its members, this anger must be released and vented. Letter writing can be the first step in expressing these strong feelings (more on this in Chapters 34 and 35). Remember, this is not about being mean to people or putting others down. The goal is healthier, more open relationships.

When you reject the old rules and uncover the myths and secrets that members invented to keep the family going, amazing things begin to happen. Close as your family may be, they may have no idea of the monsters you're carrying around with you. Just sharing the secrets of the abuse can raise your self-esteem tremendously. Hearing your family's expressions of support can be one of the most uplifting experiences of your recovery. It doesn't matter how old you are, or whether it's your parents, siblings, or your own children who are hearing the secrets. The healing process works in the same fundamental way.

One needs to use discretion when deciding what to tell children. But your children, if they are old enough, can benefit from understanding why you have been distant or irritable while you have been pursuing recovery. Also, when you share your feelings, you provide a good example of how to communicate under difficult conditions. That's a gift your children will be able to use their entire lives. Think of it as bequeathing a dove, instead of a monster, on your children's shoulders.

I once worked with the family of a Vietnam Veteran who suffered from Post-Traumatic Stress Disorder (PTSD). A powerful step in the father's recovery came when he revealed to his teenage children the wartime atrocities that he had committed. Before the session, he told me he was terrified that his children would reject him forever once they found out about his deeds, the terrible "monsters" of his past.

To their credit, the children didn't falter in their support of their father. They told him they loved him and that they understood he had acted under the terrible strain of war and that, at the time, he had felt he had no choice. The father's eyes were wide with disbelief. Then they filled with tears.

I asked him which would be more important to him, acceptance by a group of Vietnam Vets in group therapy, or acceptance by his children. Without hesitation, he said his children.

Never underestimate the value of family therapy.

26

Caution: Some Easy Pitfalls

When embarking on a new and adventurous path, it helps to expect possible obstacles along the way.

If you anticipate the challenges that lie ahead, you're in a better position to prepare for them and eventually overcome them. It's a little bit like knowing before embarking on a journey what beasts you're likely to meet in the forest. "Lions and tigers and bears, oh my!" cried Dorothy in the mythic story, *The Wizard of Oz*. Getting to your goal, whether it's the Emerald City or the serenity and self-knowledge of healing, takes persistence, vision, and most of all, courage. It can be done.

At the outset of recovery, one challenge comes from the very nature of the healing process. There's no getting around it. Recovery is change and that is hard work.

Another challenge is that therapy, though it can lead to tremendous growth, can be very painful. It may seem like a cruel twist of fate, but the deeper the trauma, the harder the work can be, especially when compounded by the survivor's feelings of extreme shame and guilt.

In cases of severe abuse, the victim probably did painful things to survive, and these memories can make a person feel especially horrible. For example, in some cases the victim may have initiated sex with the incestuous parent. The reasons are entirely understandable from the victim's point of view. Even so, the victim/survivor usually feels intense shame. The monster on their shoulder often screams in their ear that they are "no good,"

If you are a survivor, you may have done things you are ashamed of. That's okay. YOU ARE A SURVIVOR.

"worthless," "evil," "disgusting," or "the bad seed." These critical voices can drown out the person's sense of perspective and self-love. Depression, self-mutilation, and even suicide can become real risks.

If you are a survivor, you may have done things you are ashamed of. That's okay. YOU ARE A SURVIVOR. You did the best you could in an excruciating, no-win situation. It's important now that you "talk back" to the cruel monster voices that try to condemn you for your past behavior (see Chapters 34-35 on writing as therapy).

Another challenge in recovery has to do with a common internal struggle with yourself over whether you have the capacity to become an abuser yourself. It's especially critical for you to differentiate between your fear of becoming an abuser in the future and the realization that you may be one now based on your behavior. It's true that abuse survivors are at an increased risk of becoming abusers themselves. But this does not mean that you are fated to become one. It just means you need to be attentive to your feelings about the abuse and determined to work through the therapeutic process to gain a greater sense of control over your actions, i.e., rid yourself of all the monsters on your shoulder and in your closet.

It's especially critical for you to differentiate between your fear of becoming an abuser in the future and the realization that you may be one now based on your behavior.

If you are actually abusing someone right now, get immediate attention. It's important that you stop this behavior and seek professional help. Again, share your secrets. It's hard to do because of the shame involved. It's going to take guts. But it's the only way, as Ghandi put it, "to find a path out of hell."

Past abuse does not determine your destiny. For many survivors who are afraid they will become abusers themselves, this fear becomes one more monster on their shoulder.

I once worked with a 17-year-old woman who was victimized throughout her childhood. She was terrified of anyone finding out about her history, because she had heard that many victims become perpetrators themselves. She loved children but feared that people would not allow her to baby-sit if they knew she had been abused as a child. Her fear of being lumped together with perpetrators prevented her from seeking treatment sooner.

Worrying that others will assume you are unsafe simply because you were victimized as a child is another form of self-victimization. Remember that you and you alone are responsible for your behavior. You do not have to follow in the footsteps of the monster that abused you. You can walk another way.

There is another challenge that can occur during recovery. It has to do with boundary issues between patient and therapist, or between patients in a therapy group. By "boundary" I mean the line that separates the therapist and patient's lives and issues, the line that keeps the therapist a therapist and the patient a patient. Emotional sessions can affect both parties. If something feels wrong or you sense that your therapist has stepped over the line, either verbally or physically, you need to say so at the time. If that doesn't help, seek advice from an objective third party. Also see Chapters 28 and 29 which explore the kinds of monsters a therapist can bring to the treatment setting.

If you are in a group, remember that boundary issues apply here as well. It's not wise to get involved with a fellow group member. It can undermine your therapy. People who socialize together are not as open about bringing their issues, their monsters, into the group. The whole group suffers when the emotional and behavioral boundaries that form a positive structure for therapy break down. Using group as a resource for friendship or romance also corrodes the therapeutic process. It leaves you dependent on the group to form new relationships. The group is for learning how to make friends, or to be a better friend, to bolster your relationships outside the group.

27

The Role of Medication

During the recovery process, if you feel overwhelmed with rage, grief, or other strong emotion that interferes with your functioning on a daily basis, then you may wish to consider the possibility of taking medication.

Seeking temporary relief through medication does not mean that you are a quitter. This kind of punitive thought sounds like the voices of your monster. Considering medication means that you are concerned for your well-being and are exploring every avenue to get well.

> Seeking temporary relief through medication does not mean that you are a quitter. This kind of punitive thought sounds like the voices of your monster.

Similarly, if your therapist recommends medication and refers you to a psychiatrist, this doesn't mean your therapist isn't listening to you or is shunting you off onto someone else. The recommendation for medication can be part of a sincere effort to help relieve your suffering.

As an M.D., I have learned when psychotherapy can be helpful, and when medications can be helpful. I am not a pill-pusher, but I let patients know that medication is an option available to them as they proceed with extremely painful work. That is also my purpose here: to give you the facts so you can be an informed participant in this aspect of the treatment process. The final decision of whether to take medication and what kind to take is a personal matter between you and your therapist or psychiatrist.

Wild emotional roller-coaster swings can be symptoms of an underlying mood disorder, or a cry for help. If a patient feels suicidal, so depressed that he can't get out of bed in the morning, so irritable that he's having trouble functioning at work, or so enraged that he's afraid he'll physically abuse his own children, then medication may be extremely valuable.

Without going into great detail about all the medications available to you, let me outline the basic types of drugs and some of their benefits and drawbacks.

Antidepressants can be helpful if you are depressed or anxious. There are different types of antidepressants, some with more side effects than others. Contrary to the negative publicity surrounding Prozac, I have found it to be an effective drug in the treatment of both serious and chronic mild depression. Zoloft and Paxil are similar to Prozac. The tricyclic antidepressants (such as Imiprimine) are especially helpful if you suffer from panic attacks or Attention Deficit Disorder.

Medications such as Lithium can be useful for people suffering from volatile mood swings or intense, persistent anger. Lithium and the antidepressants are commonly used together without significant drug interaction.

The well-known antianxiety drugs such as Valium and Xanax (the family of drugs known as benzo-diazepines) can be risky because of the potential for physical addiction. If prescribed, these drugs should be monitored carefully.

Y ou have a right to knowledge before taking any kind of drug.

Antipsychotic medications, also called neuroleptics (such as Haldol, Thorazine, and Prolixin), can have serious long-term side effects. In my view, these drugs should be used only after other methods of treatment are exhausted. However, under the right circumstances they can be very effective at helping to relieve suffering.

Before you take any medication, you deserve to be informed of the potential short-term and long-term risks and benefits. This is called "Informed Consent." It is a basic principle of fairness. It means that you have a right to knowledge before taking any kind of drug. Remember, you deserve to have this information, and to have your questions answered fully and openly.

How do you obtain medication? If you are currently in treatment, ask your therapist for a referral to a psychiatrist for a consultation to discuss possible use of medication. This can be a one-time visit and does not necessarily require that you continue to see the psychiatrist on a regular basis.

If you are not in treatment but would like to be, and if you are considering using medication, it might be best to consult a psychiatrist at the outset, preferably one who is experienced with recovery from abuse. Because of the complex relationship between symptoms, medication, and underlying emotional or physical problems, I recommend consulting a psychiatrist rather than another type of doctor. Your family practitioner, internist, or gynecologist are good sources for a referral.

Is medication a permanent solution? That depends on you and your unique path through recovery. Often, medications can lessen the suffering and pain that comes when you have memories of the abuse. They can help stabilize mood swings or depressions, and they can lessen the seriousness, frequency, or duration of relapses.

Medications can play an important part in helping you tolerate the symptoms of pain so that you can continue with the necessary psychotherapy without having to go through excruciating pain and suffering.

Once psychotherapy has had a chance to take root, and you have had the opportunity to do some of the work involved in facing your monsters and exploring your emotions and memories, you may be able to reduce or stop the medications altogether.

Many people who have suffered abuse find relief from learning meditation and self-hypnosis. I have seen cases where these proved to be even more helpful than medications, particularly those medications with potentially serious side effects. In Part 4, I offer a variety of behavior exercises and relaxation therapies that you can practice on your own. You may find that these methods work so well you won't need medication to handle the stresses of life and the hard, but rewarding, work of recovery.

28

Therapists Can Have Monsters, Too

Most therapists are well-meaning, conscientious people who are dedicated to their profession and to the healing of others. However, even the most conscientious doctors can make mistakes. Unfortunately sometimes there are situations that arise where a therapist allows his or her needs to take precedence over those of the patient. If the therapist does not take care of the problem, it can undermine or even destroy the patient-therapist relationship.

> One of the most common ways a therapist can dump a "monster" on a patient is to become involved in a power struggle.

In other words, beware the therapist who lets his or her monsters leap from their shoulders into the treatment room.

One of the most common ways a therapist can dump a "monster" on a patient is to become involved in a power struggle. It is important for a therapist to avoid arguing with patients over the cost, order, or intensity of the recovery.

I learned this lesson the hard way during my early days as a resident in psychiatry, the last phase of my formal training before starting my practice.

At that time, I had a male patient who seemed to reject every good idea I had. My supervisor required me to tape record all the sessions and play portions of them back to her during supervisory meetings. During one session, my supervisor pointed out that she could tell from the tone of my voice that I was getting angry at the patient. She had to play that portion of the tape about four times until I understood what she was getting at. She helped me to see that the session had deteriorated from that point on.

As my supervisor and I talked, I was able to identify my anger and perceive the damage that it was doing to the treatment. Nevertheless, I still found it hard to understand why I was reacting in that way.

For this patient's next session, I came prepared with a pad and pen to take notes on why I was becoming angry with him. Much to my surprise, and benefit, I became aware of the thoughts popping into my head as I began to get angry. These spontaneous thoughts helped to explain my anger. I saw that I was irritated at this man because (as I was experiencing it), he would not take my advice, he would not get well fast enough, and he would not take the medications that I was sure would improve his moods and allow him to recapture his lost energy and direction.

I realized, too, that I wanted to impress my supervisor with the stellar progress of my patient. In other words, I found myself feeling emotionally dependent on this man. For me to be a "good" psychiatrist, he had to get better. For me to feel successful in my work, I needed this poor guy to accept all my advice, agree with all my interpretations, and get well quickly.

What a monster I was placing on his shoulder!

After that point, the best thing I did for him (and indirectly for myself) was to ask a simple question: "Why do you continue to come here week after week, subjecting yourself to these control struggles?"

It turned out that he kept coming back precisely because we were having control struggles and because he felt he was winning every single one of them. He felt that repeatedly winning these struggles with a person such as myself (a doctor, a professional) meant that he was strong. The fact that his treatment was going nowhere was of little concern to him. After talking it over we agreed that a vacation from therapy might be useful so that he could decide for himself what he really wished to accomplish.

Since then, I have always tried to make sure my

goals for my patients are more focused on what they want to accomplish for themselves. If a patient has no goal, then a vacuum exists. I know from experience that such a vacuum is like an empty cave which I could all too easily fill with my own monsters, if I'm not careful. This is neither healthy nor constructive. In these cases I simply draw on all the patience I can muster, and allow the patient to set the direction in his or her own time.

Thus, beware if you and your therapist become engaged in a struggle for control.

There is also another kind of monster that is even more serious. This is when the therapist "crosses the line" and acts in a seductive or romantic way with a patient.

Though not obvious on the surface, this kind of violation usually also stems from a struggle for control or power. Instead of realizing what's happening and staying focused on the patient's needs, the therapist steps out of the role of healer and takes on the face of the monster. That is, the doctor preys on the vulnerability of the patient.

Next we'll look at two stories that show what happens when monsters rule the therapeutic practice.

29

Monsters in a Safe Place Unsafe Boundaries

The ultimate violation of the "safe place" that therapy should be is when a therapist and patient have a sexual relationship. Sadly, it is becoming more and more common to hear this kind of story. It's a serious problem and harmful to the patient. The American Medical Association has declared that such relationships are unprofessional and cannot be allowed. It is absolutely taboo among all reputable mental health professionals.

The bond between a patient and a physician, psychiatrist, or any other type of therapist, is a relationship based on trust for the health and benefit of the patient, not for the personal or sexual gratification of the therapist. The mixture of sex and therapy destroys the therapeutic work and often causes the patient to relive feelings of sexual exploitation and emotional injury from the past.

I'd like to share two stories that demonstrate this point.

The first is the story of Becky, a 29-year-old married woman who came to me for treatment due to problems in her marriage, panic attacks, and depression. She had recently terminated her work with another psychiatrist. In our early sessions she said that her reason for terminating the other treatment was that she felt she was falling in love with the therapist. Later, however, she revealed that she felt he had encouraged her to sit on his lap during a session. She had recognized and struggled with her sexual and extramarital fantasies about this therapist, but began to fear that he could not control his impulses any longer.

Becky had a complex history that explains her pattern of destructive relationships. She was the youngest of eight children, and during her childhood she was neglected by her mother and workaholic father. Her self-esteem was very low. As a teenager she was drawn to any boy who would show her attention. Beatings and episodes of date rape were not uncommon for her. Tragically, sexual and physical violence became a necessary tradeoff for her in order to feel desired and wanted. As an adult she married a man who basically ignored her, just as her father had done.

During Becky's work with me, something happened that helped us examine the issue of sexual and erotic issues between patients and therapists. At the end of a session, I realized I had accidentally double-booked appointments for the next week. I asked Becky to reschedule her appointment. She became very angry with me. In fact, she slammed the door on her way out and phoned several times, leaving messages on my answering machine in which she expressed her hurt feelings.

On the day of the rescheduled session, she was dressed conservatively in a flowered dress. She later told me that she had bought a very sexy top with the intention of wearing it to the session. This allowed us to talk about the connection between her anger and her sexuality. At this point, Becky mentioned that her husband was more frequently out of town on business, another source of her anger and feelings of neglect. We discussed her feelings for her previous psychiatrist and looked for similar patterns with other men she fantasized and "obsessed about" (her phrase). Becky realized that a struggle for power was a common denominator in these relationships and fantasies.

This was particularly true when it came to her previous experiences in treatment. Becky had felt sexual feelings toward many of her doctors. She recited a list of four or five of them. I noticed that I was not on the list. When I commented on this, she said that though she had obsessed about me, she felt I was different because I was the only one she thought was not attracted to her.

The more we talked, the more it became clear that these other doctors had acted in inappropriate, highly sexualized ways. One in particular had stared at her legs throughout their first meeting while he was taking her medical history and discussing her problems. Becky had terminated her work with her previous psychiatrist when she felt he was speaking seductively to her, suggesting that some women often feel as though they would like to be hugged or to sit on a man's lap. Although she had strong feelings for this man, Becky ended the work because she did not believe that he could control his desires if she succumbed to hers.

This was a healthy move on her part. The price of such a liaison would have been devastating. I asked Becky how she would compare the pain of such a relationship with her psychiatrist to previous sexual and physical abuse by boyfriends. She said that she had been forced by a number of men (more than she had previously stated) to have sex against her will. That had been painful enough, yet she felt that sex with her therapist would have been far more traumatic. In fact, she stated that she probably would have felt like committing suicide if it had occurred.

At the end of the session I offered my hand for what I termed "a respectful handshake." We shook hands and the session ended. Becky looked more confident and pleased with herself. I think the handshake was therapeutic. After that session, Becky was more assertive in treatment, and her self-esteem and confidence grew steadily.

When treatment reinforces respectful boundaries, the therapist is saying to the patient, "I respect you and I will not use you to further my own pleasure. I will keep my monsters to myself." Conversely, when the therapist crosses the line, it can undermine everything treatment is supposed to do. The patient can't look at her own problems because the therapist's own monsters are taking precedence.

For Pamela, a 35-year-old woman, this was the case. I met Pamela in the course of working with her 11-year-old son. Behavioral management training was not going well and I met privately with Pamela to discuss the lack of progress. I quickly realized that Pamela was very depressed, so I pursued this issue for a while to find out what was preventing her from establishing fairly straightforward limits with her son.

Pamela said she was in treatment with a local psychiatrist and on medication. When she began to talk about her relationship with her therapist, it became clear that boundaries had been violated.

She said it had begun one day when she had arrived beaming with excitement. The psychiatrist asked if she was having an affair. She said no. He asked if she had a crush on somebody. She said yes. He asked who it was, and she told him that it was him. At this point, the doctor got down on his knees in front of her and said, "I would love to make love to you. But if I did then I couldn't help you."

After that "noble" act (which I consider seductive and manipulative), the sexual current in their relationship became more intense. Pamela reported that she had often spent sessions sitting on the doctor's lap. They would kiss and cuddle, as part of the therapy, he said. He placed his hands up her legs, though he never touched her genitalia.

Pamela was content to continue this relationship until a close friend of hers, who was also seeing the same doctor, confided to her that similar things were happening in her treatment. Pamela felt very hurt. She had believed she was the only one her therapist cared for in this way.

She became distraught, and her depression grew worse. She told her husband about "the affair," as she called it, and he was deeply hurt. In fact, after learning about his wife's involvement with her doctor, he became suicidal on at least two different occasions. Once, he drove his car at very high speeds, intending to crash it. During another episode he placed his revolver to his head, yearning to pull the trigger. Their young son was out of control, but Pamela and her husband were so preoccupied with their own issues that they could not address their son's needs.

The tragedy of this kind of violation is that the experience is very akin to incest. Trust is betrayed, and the victim can feel humiliated and debased. Self-blame, guilt, and shame almost always result. Often, victims of childhood abuse are the most vulnerable to this type of exploitation. They go to a therapist for help. Instead they are violated once again. Regression is common when today's experiences resemble yesterday's exploitation.

I am not telling these stories to frighten you or to imply that this is likely to happen to you if you seek professional help. Rather, I share them in an effort to raise your awareness.

> If you think that something's wrong, but you don't know what it is, you're probably right. Trust yourself.

When you're in recovery, feelings can be complex and confusing. It is an intense experience, and it can be easy to doubt yourself and what you feel. The therapist's job is to help you understand your feelings; not to act them out with you. A skilled therapist helps you clarify feelings, helps you separate one strand from another.

For example, when I worked with Becky we discussed her sexual attraction to her previous therapist. I explained that many people experience anxiety as erotic arousal, and that the challenge is to learn how to read these feelings as anxiety rather than sexual interest. Becky agreed that anxiety over the power difference between her and the doctor is what made her feel "excited," which led her to think about sexual matters rather than the bigger issues such as her low self-esteem or the doctor's inappropriate sexualization of their relationship.

What do you do if something is happening in treatment which you feel may be sexual abuse? First, talk about it with your therapist. Explain what is distressing you. If that doesn't help, or if your therapist is unresponsive, talk to a third party. Consult a family doctor, or other person whom you trust. In other words just as we say to kids when we teach about "good touching" and "bad touching" if you feel you are being abused, "tell someone." If you think that something's wrong, but you don't know what it is, you're probably right. Trust yourself.

Therapy can be a transforming and very energizing process. You are entitled to receive help, not harm. This means having the healing attention of a therapist who knows how to control his or her "inner monster." It means finding support and empathy. It means your need to heal is the top priority, before all other needs.

As a person in recovery, a person standing up to say, "I am a human being, I do not deserve to be exploited," you deserve nothing less than that.

Part 4

Healing Techniques & Exercises

30

The Monster and the Invisible Electric Fence

Have you ever heard of the invisible electric fence used to keep dogs in their yards?

An electric wire is buried underground, and the dog wears a special collar around its neck. If the dog tries to cross the electric field, the collar delivers an electric shock to the animal. Fearing the pain of that electric shock, the dog learns to stay inside the invisible fence. It yearns to break free, to leave the confines of the yard, to explore the world outside, but the electric shock delivers a choke-hold reminder every time the animal tries to escape.

On the other hand, say the dog sees another dog outside the yard with whom it wants to mate. It runs full speed toward the invisible fence. The jolt of the electric shock hurts, but by this time sheer momentum has carried the dog through the fence. Only after it lands on the other side does the dog actually become aware of the pain. Now you've got one angry beast, but it's free. Once the dog breaks through the barrier, it can go anywhere it wants except back to that small jail-cell of a yard.

The same pattern can occur in the mind of an abuse survivor. Abuse can cause people to feel confined within a small area in their minds. Memories of abuse hurt so much that people do everything they can to avoid them. Like an electric jolt, the stabbing pain keeps them from exploring, understanding, and moving beyond the terrible experiences of the past.

Memories of abuse hurt so much that people do everything they can to avoid them.

In a sense, the pain itself becomes a kind of monster. Recovery requires remembering and confronting the memories as much as possible. But the "invisible electric fence" in the survivor's mind, that circle of pain ringed around the nightmare, keeps people from doing the necessary work. The memory arises, the shock comes, and the person retreats inward again, hiding from the painful recollections. When this occurs, the survivor feels powerless and fearful, like a victim again.

Recalling the memories of abuse, whether it happened when the person was a child, teenager, or adult, can be very traumatic. The images and words recalled can be terrifying. The survivor can feel overwhelming disgust, shame, guilt, fear, and loneliness. Flashbacks, visual images of traumatic experiences, can occur like a moving picture telling a terrible story. The person experiences the images in real time, as if watching a television show. The flashbacks may also include physical sensations, further intensifying the feeling that it's all happening in the present.

For example, a person who was forced to perform fellatio with an abuser may feel overwhelming nausea, or may have uncomfortable sensations in the mouth, throat, or stomach. That person might not even be able to eat without throwing up afterwards.

Dissociation, or a feeling of being not connected to the present, can also occur. In dissociative episodes, the whole experience of reality at that moment is altered. The person, seeing images of past trauma or abuse, can become temporarily transported back to that time and believe he is experiencing the abuse at that very moment. Hugs or supportive physical touches by loved ones can be perceived as touches from the perpetrator. This invisible electric fence keeps the victim locked inside.

What is needed is a means of getting through the electric fence without triggering overwhelming and terrifying symptoms. Many survivors of abuse need to find ways to soothe and calm themselves, to learn how to go through the necessary steps in the arduous but liberating process of recovery. It means staring down the monster of pain and turning it into a less terrifying kind of beast, one that can be negotiated with, compromised with, made less threatening.

There are some excellent relaxation, self-hypnosis, and meditation techniques that can be helpful in soothing that monstrous pain or neutralizing the electric fence. These methods are helpful because they calm you in the present. They provide respite from thoughts of the past (which result in depression) or the future (which can trigger

> Learning how to relax, soothe the pain,
> and reassure yourself is like learning how to
> hold your own hand as you cross the yard
> and open the door to the world outside.

anxiety and fear). By staying in the present, you give yourself precious moments of life free from the monsters on your shoulder.

In the next few chapters I'll introduce you to some of these techniques. I hope you will learn them, practice them, and add other methods that you have found helpful.

Today, relaxation, self-hypnosis, and meditation techniques are being used by many people as a simple way of coping with tension. I believe abuse survivors can benefit from using these techniques as well. Learning how to relax, soothe the pain, and reassure yourself is like learning how to hold your own hand as you cross the yard and open the door to the world outside. You become your own caretaker.

Whether you choose yoga, meditation, self-hypnosis, soothing music, creative acts such as writing or drawing, or some other healthy activity, these various ways of affirming yourself will help you heal. With these techniques, you won't feel the desperate need to retreat whenever you approach your inner barriers to recovery and freedom.

31

Soothing Techniques

We all need to find ways to manage stress. However, survivors have a special challenge. Often they must confront some very unhappy memories in their quest for serenity and wholeness. The soothing techniques I'm about to present can be a kind of "monster antidote" for when the pain and terror begin to feel overwhelming.

Controlled Breathing

The essence of life is breath. The flow of life is like the inhale/exhale rhythms of the body. As you develop a gentle sense of mastery over your breathing, the more likely you are to feel that you, not your abuser, "own" your own body. It is like coming home to yourself, to your first, deepest source of life.

Controlled breathing is a wonderful relaxation technique. It's simple, effective, and absolutely free. Here's how it works:

First, open your jaw slightly. Your lips can be open or closed. Put the tip of your tongue against the roof of your mouth, just behind your front teeth.

Next, breathe slowly and deeply through your nose. Inhale and exhale slowly. Your mind will become calmer. Keep breathing this way for as long as you like, but try to stay with it for at least a couple of minutes.

Do you notice you can hear the air flowing through your nostrils? You'll probably find that your hearing and other senses become more acute as you breathe in and out.

As you develop a gentle sense of mastery over your breathing, the more likely you are to feel that you, not your abuser, "own" your own body.

There are several reasons why this simple technique works so well. First, opening the jaw just a bit produces instant relaxation in your jaw muscles. We often react to tension by clenching our teeth. Catch yourself in the middle of a tense moment one day and see if your jaw isn't held tighter than usual. When you open the jaw slightly, the relaxation is not confined to these muscles only, but affects your entire body.

This gentle exercise of slow, deep breathing has a direct physiological effect on the body. It lowers the carbon dioxide levels in the blood, which can reduce perceptions of pain. Also, slow, deep breathing is the opposite of the body's normal response to panic. During panic attacks, people often breathe in a rapid, shallow fashion. Guiding your body to do the opposite tells the body "I am calm, I am not afraid, I am okay."

This technique can be used any time, but it's especially helpful when you are feeling anxious or overwhelmed. It can also be incorporated into other exercises or activities that you do, like yoga, walking, or jogging, for a more peaceful feeling. It doesn't cost a dime and it's totally under your control.

Meditation

Meditation is a terrific technique that can help you regain self-control and serenity. I am not an expert on meditation. In fact, I'm just a beginner in the practice myself. However, I have come to appreciate meditation as a highly effective method of cognitive (thinking) therapy. It's a great way to practice "thought interruption" or "blocking."

Meditation can help you temporarily replace negative and painful thoughts with a positive, uplifting experience of life. This doesn't mean the pain goes away entirely, but meditation can provide a brief reprieve from the pain. You can gain a little perspective, find your footing, reassure yourself that things aren't always bleak and that there is hope.

A meditation technique that I have found helpful is a Buddhist method called "Loving Kindness." All you do is get comfortable, practice your controlled breathing, and repeat a series of statements in your mind. As you repeat the statements, you visualize whoever it is you're addressing at the moment.

The steps are listed below. Each one takes about 5 minutes, for a total of 30-35 minutes. Try to allow yourself at least 30 minutes to complete the whole exercise.

As you repeat each statement, picture the person(s) in your mind, as if you were really talking to them. (A few visualizations tips are included in parentheses.)

1. "May I be happy and well." (Visualize yourself happy and well.)

2. "May [someone you love, like, or respect] be happy and well." (This could be your spouse, child, friend, or co-worker.)

3. "May [someone you feel neutral towards] be happy and well." (For example, the mail carrier, a grocery clerk.)

4. "May [someone you dislike or hate] be happy and well." (This is the hard part. Perhaps this will be someone who has hurt you, made you angry, or let you down. Or, if you can do it, perhaps this will be your abuser. There's

144

no "right" or "wrong" choice. Focus on whomever you want to at the moment.)

5. "May [everyone in the above 4 steps] be happy and well. May we all be happy and well." (When I do this step, I like to envision that all of us are standing in a group waiting to have our picture taken. Our arms are on each other's shoulders, and we're smiling into the camera. I see everyone standing together, feeling warmly toward each other, and a good feeling washes over me, even toward the person I dislike or hate.)

6. "May the community be happy and well." (You could picture everyone on your block, in your neighborhood, or in your town.)

7. "May the world be happy and well." (Perhaps picture our fragile globe, spinning in space, and all the people whose lives are so interwoven in the world hand in hand looking up at the stars.)

When you have completed all seven steps, you'll find you feel relaxed, with warm, positive feelings surging through you. Practicing this exercise on a regular basis can change the way you view yourself and others. It's also a great thought interrupter when negative, painful, or angry feelings threaten to swamp all other emotions.

Spending even just 15 minutes a day on this

exercise can prove helpful. You'll be amazed by how this small investment of time can reduce the amount of time you spend obsessing negatively about life and the past.

People often have a hard time with Step 4. You don't have to start off by envisioning your perpetrator. While some survivors find this is the ultimate balm to their wounded souls (see Chapter 42 on forgiveness), it's fine to start out with the image of someone you just don't like very much. If you never move on to picture your abuser, that's alright. Remember, this meditation is for your benefit only, no one else's. It's a private experience. What you think about is totally up to you.

Feel free to modify the exercise to suit your personal needs and interests. I like the exercise as it is, but I trust you to come up with your own version that may work even better for you.

32

Self-Hypnosis

Self-hypnosis is an outstanding method for reducing the intensity of the "electric fence," described in Chapter 30, as you approach your monsters in your mind and memory. With practice, you can learn to use it when you have horrible memories and flashbacks, or to simply relax or tolerate unpleasant situations (a boring lecture, waiting in the dentist's office). Common sense will govern where and when you choose to do the exercise. However, don't risk your physical safety by attempting it while driving when you need to concentrate.

As you practice this technique, you can develop your own style and approach. You need not feel there is only one way to do it.

Here's how I like to structure the exercise:

First, start with three controlled breaths. (Tip of your tongue on the roof of your mouth, jaw slightly open, breathe slowly and deeply.) Almost instantly you will begin to feel more relaxed. Continue with the controlled breathing throughout the rest of the exercise.

Now roll your eyes up into the top of your head, then close your eyes. At this point, picture yourself going either up or down.

Some people like to picture themselves on an elevator or escalator. (I like to picture the escalators in the Washington, D.C., subway. They're the longest and deepest I've ever seen. A parachute is also a favorite image for the sensation of going down. Or, you can imagine yourself floating upwards. Many people envision floating up to a cloud, or into the darkness of outer space. Again, any choice is fine.

Check your breathing at this point to be sure you are still breathing slowly and deeply. Now, as you imagine yourself going down or up, speak to yourself internally in a soft, soothing voice. Tell yourself that you are going up (or down), getting more relaxed, going higher (deeper, farther), and feeling safer. As you do this, you'll feel more relaxed and safe.

When you feel ready, you will mentally travel to your "safe place." A safe place can be any place where you feel absolutely safe. The image will be as unique as you are. Many people choose a beach, the woods, or a high mountaintop. One young man I know chose his father's boat. A bedroom can feel safe for many (though not for others).

One woman who has survived a serious heart attack feels safe only in an Intensive Care Unit bed, so that's where she goes in her self-hypnosis.

The goal is simply to go to a place in your mind where there is absolutely, positively, no question that you will feel safe. It's the place where no monsters can find you.

When going to your safe place, you can literally travel to it. When you have reached the bottom of the escalator or elevator ride, you can get into a car and travel to your safe place.

Picture yourself travelling to your safe place, going down to the bottom of the escalator or way up to the top of the elevator ride. Drive to your safe place. Park the car. Open the door and get out. Now walk to your destination. Enter your safe place, sit down on a bench or chair and continue with your slow, deep breaths. Look around you and tell yourself about the place where you're sitting, the look, feel, and touch of the room. If your safe place is outdoors, sit on the grass or in some other comfortable spot. Describe the surroundings to yourself. For example, tell yourself the temperature is perfect, the sky is blue, there is a gentle breeze, the sea gulls are flying about, the air smells great. Let yourself be playful. If you floated up to a cloud, for example, you might sail down to your safe place. Or the cloud itself could be your safe place.

Wherever you are, just enjoy it. Stay there as long as you like. Continue with the controlled breathing and just enjoy yourself. You deserve this relief from stress and suffering.

When you're ready to come out of the hypnosis exercise, mentally count backwards from five to one. As you do this, you will feel as if you are getting lighter and lighter. When you reach the count of one, open your eyes. If you feel tired, you can close your eyes and return to your safe place. Then, when you're ready, count yourself out of the exercise a second time. Remember, you are totally in control of this process. You go where you want to go, get there by whatever means you choose, and stay there as long as you like. You are in control, from the feel of the air to the look of the sand and sky.

A wonderful thing about this relaxation method is that it can help you "cross the invisible electric fence" without experiencing the usual shock and pain. It can become a way for you to face the monsters in your mind without feeling over-whelmed. Let's say you've just come home from a very painful therapy session. You feel so much despair that you don't know how you'll go on. You can use this wonderful exercise to help you recall a sense of your own personal freedom, power, and value. It's like a little "breathing space" that allows you to face painful feelings without being victimized again or retreating inwards and running from your recovery work.

This may seem like a lot of mental steps at first, but in time, and with practice, the technique can become almost automatic.

To review, here's a quick checklist of the steps in the self-hypnosis exercise:

1. Controlled breathing.
2. Roll your eyes up into your head.
3. Close your eyes.
4. Imagine yourself going up or down.
5. Imagine yourself becoming calmer, going higher, deeper, farther, more relaxed, feeling safer.

One of the beauties of the self-hypnosis exercise is that it allows you to find a safe place·on your own. You don't need anybody else to help you get to your safe place. It costs nothing, and it can be tremendously liberating.

6. When you feel very relaxed and safe, travel to your special safe place.
7. Describe your safe place to yourself. Describe how you feel in your safe place.
8. Stay in your safe place for as long as you like.

9. Leave the safe place. End the exercise by counting backwards from 5 to 1.
10. Sit for a moment and feel what you feel.

Note: If you get distracted during the exercise, focus on the distraction. You will then be able to return to the exercise.

One final note: Remember what I said about how therapy should be a safe place? One of the beauties of the self-hypnosis exercise is that it allows you to find a safe place on your own. You don't need anybody else to help you get to your safe place. It costs nothing, and it can be tremendously liberating. I hope you will consider adopting it as one of your allies in the recovery process.

33

Visualizations

A visualization exercise I like to use is one called the "Split-Screen Technique."

This exercise involves imagining yourself in a movie theater with two screens. One of the screens is for warm, soothing images. The other screen is for upsetting, painful images.

Envision yourself sitting comfortably in a seat of your own choosing. You have a remote-control switch in each hand, allowing you to choose instantly between either screen.

Start with the positive screen. (I like to put it on my left side, but you're free to choose either position.) When you feel ready, switch to the negative screen and introduce a troubling image. As soon as it feels too overwhelming, switch back to the soothing screen.

After calming yourself and when you feel ready, switch back to the negative screen. Stay there as long as you can without feeling overwhelmed, then switch back to the positive screen. Adjust the volume as you go.

What you're doing with this exercise is essentially desensitizing yourself from painful memories. This is different from experiencing frightening or terrifying memories and retreating inward. Here, you are continually developing and perfecting a method for gaining control. Pulling away from the negative material quickly and moving back and forth entirely at your own will enhance rather than hinder your feelings of power and self-control.

Many patients find that the process makes them feel stronger and more confident. They feel less afraid of the past and of the monsters on their shoulder.

You can try this exercise whenever you feel you need to boost your bravery and courage.

34

Writing as Therapy

Writing as therapy involves using one of your most creative abilities to express how you feel. Writing is a powerful way to release emotions, to deal with memories, unresolved issues, and to find the strength you need to handle difficult times in your present life.

You don't have to be a published writer to do this. You don't even have to think of yourself as a "good writer." People of all ages and all backgrounds find writing helpful for getting out their feelings.

One of the great things about writing is that it creates a permanent record. Something written on the spur of the moment, in a time of emotional upset, is valuable right then. But it can also be useful days, months, or even years later in helping you chart your path in recovery. Looking back, you can see just how far you have come, as a person and as a survivor. You can also gain insight into yourself and those recurring emotional patterns that you wish to keep working on.

Most of all, writing, like all creative acts, is expressive. Expression is something that many abuse survivors were denied as children. Often their voices were stunted or even stifled forever. Some incest victims, for example, became completely mute as a result of the horrors they experienced.

The human voice, with its sound, rhythms, and flow, is one of the instruments we use to reach out to others and make contact. Our words, sentences, paragraphs connect us to others and make us feel less alone.

Many people are surprised and delighted to find that in the act of writing they realize something they didn't know before or had forgotten.

Writing is a process of discovery. Many people are surprised and delighted to find that in the act of writing they realize something they didn't know before or had forgotten. At the moment of discovery, things come together, a light shines, feelings crystallize, and a new pattern emerges.

Writing can be private or public. As a private act, it is beautiful because nobody but you need read what you write. As a victim, your privacy was most likely invaded in many different ways. For you, the power and beauty of writing might be that you finally have a private space, a safe place, where you can express your thoughts. You and only you control them. You and only you will read the words, unless you choose to share them with others.

Let me give you an example of how writing therapy worked for one young woman who had been sexually assaulted. Several months after this patient had experienced an acquaintance rape, I commented on how well she had handled the trauma. She seemed remarkably strong and healthy. Her demeanor was even more striking because I remembered how she had been a year before—a timid college student wanting everyone to like her.

I asked her what she thought had made it possible for her to recover from this trauma so well, especially compared to how she might have handled it a year earlier. She said two things had made a big difference for her. First, during the therapy session just prior to the assault, she had decided to write letters to men in her past who had hurt her. She was going to write to an ex-boyfriend and to her father. But before she could write the letters, the sexual assault occurred. After the attack, she decided to write a letter to the perpetrator instead of the two men from her past. It was a very powerful letter. Through the vehicle of the letter, she took the monster of sexual abuse that temporarily had found a home on her shoulder and transferred it to a piece of paper. She then was able to see it more clearly, and she refused to accept it.

She didn't stop there, however. She shared with friends what had happened, using the letter as a springboard to talk about her feelings.

Feel free to use the exercises in the next chapter as a starting point for your own creative exploration of your past, present, and future. Invent new and different writing exercises that occur to you. Follow your instincts. And remember, no one need read these writings but you. As a popular movie theme song put it, they're "for your eyes only."

The writing exercises provide you with one more tool for your growing arsenal of beast-busting techniques.

Three Success Stories: Ways to Use Writing as Therapy

People have their own ways of healing, and people have their own ways of using writing as therapy. I'd like to share with you the following three anecdotes, each one the story of a courageous young woman.

The first one is about Sally, whom you met in Chapter Five and who had so much trouble talking about her anger and pain because of her Learned Powerlessness. I'd like to show you how she used writing as a way of finding a voice, not just as a person who writes, but as a person recovering from abuse.

Bonnie and Robin also used writing to overcome their pain and their problems. I hope their stories will encourage you to find your own way of using writing as therapy.

Sally's Story

You may remember from Chapter Five that Sally was the 10-year-old girl who was abused and then abandoned by her biological father. At the time I met her after her hospitalization, she was having an ongoing problem with her stepfather. Sally felt he was verbally abusive and that he liked to hurt and humiliate her. Sally also felt betrayed by her mother, who seemed to take sides against her.

Sally was furious, but unable to talk about it. Instead she took to punching holes in walls and attacking her mother and brother.

Working with Sally proved difficult at first. In therapy, she "hit the wall" when she tried to confront her pain. She just couldn't voice her feelings to her stepfather. The Learned Powerlessness was too deep.

While I thought it would be helpful for her to confront her stepfather, Sally wanted nothing to do with that. All she wanted was to live someplace other than home. I saw the chance for her to work through her feelings in a letter, but she just couldn't do it.

She did try one thing, though. When I suggested she draw a picture of the monster on her shoulder, she picked up a crayon. She proceeded to draw a picture of herself as a very stunted little girl with a huge monster on her shoulder. In the drawing, Sally was tiny and the monster was enormous. Here, I thought, was a beginning, and a clue: Sally felt so dwarfed by her stepfather that she couldn't imagine talking to him. She was terrified.

I did my best to encourage and support Sally through her fears, but her mind was made up. She wanted to be placed in residential foster care.

I began to think that, in Sally's case, 10 years of age might be just too young for her to handle all the work of therapy. Perhaps the best we could hope for would be a breakthrough at an older age.

But then, to my surprise, we got lucky.

Sally took the initiative one day and wrote a short letter to her stepfather. In the letter, she talked about some of her most painful memories, experiences she'd shared with me but never with her parents. This letter represented genuine progress, the first step in Sally's healing.

The next weekend, on a pass from the hospital, Sally had a chance to talk to her mother. Sally told her mother about one painful memory when her stepfather accused her of deliberately getting chicken pox on the day of his marriage to Sally's mother. For the first time, Sally told her mother how hurt she was by his accusation. Her mother consoled her, but then she explained that Sally's stepfather had himself had a very hard life. When he was very young, he'd lost his own father. It was a deep and painful wound.

To her credit, Sally let this sink in. She was able to feel compassion for her stepfather, though she was still angry at him. The next day, when Sally went out with her mother and stepfather, it was more pleasant, more like she imagined a family should be.

When I learned of Sally's success, I was delighted for her. However, I felt it was very important for her to talk directly with her stepfather, while the feelings were still fresh and the family unity stronger. I suggested she might want to call him. To my surprise, she did.

Here's what she said: "I was hurt when you blamed me for having chicken pox. I thought you didn't love me. I just want you to know that . . . I want to go home." Success. Mission accomplished. Just letting him know how she felt was true success.

We arranged another pass for that day, and that went well, too. Sally's stepfather apologized. Then he talked about how painful his childhood had been. He had been physically abused by a father who eventually abandoned the family. Now, here was real sharing in a family that had been so torn apart.

Sally finally went home and made the transition nicely. I haven't heard of any problems since. Looking back now, I can see the value of writing as a first tiny step. I think that, once Sally saw she had something to say, by writing it in a letter, she gained the confidence and motivation to "find her voice" in other ways. The steps went something like this:

- Sally says nothing ("hits the wall")
- Sally writes a letter to her stepfather but doesn't mail it (success)
- Sally talks to her mother (more success)
- Sally talks to her stepfather (still more success)
- Sally's stepfather apologizes and talks openly with Sally about his own painful childhood ("icing on the cake")

Although she was only 10, Sally was able to free herself from many of the "monsters on her shoulder," most of all, from her Learned Powerlessness.

Bonnie's Story

When she was only two years old, Bonnie was abandoned by her neglectful, physically abusive and chemically addicted mother, so Bonnie's biological father took her in. Not one for steady relationships, he married two more times, and had many girlfriends in between the marriages.

Bonnie's father also had a temper, and physical abuse became a regular event for Bonnie.

Bonnie often fed into this cycle by provoking her father. She found it hard to voice her anger directly. Instead, she acted out or dumped her anger on her stepmother. The stepmother then complained to Bonnie's father who reacted by getting angry and hitting Bonnie. A triangle developed. The monster that was Dad's abuse weighed heavily on Bonnie. She threw the monster at Mom, who was less intimidating and frightening. Then Mom gave it to Dad, who dumped it back on Bonnie. Everyone ended up with monsters to deal with and nobody won.

To their credit, Bonnie's father and stepmother were able to perceive some of the craziness of this dynamic, and they sought therapy. Remarkably, before the first session, Bonnie took an important step. Without realizing it, she initiated her own healing by getting started on a letter. Here is her letter:

A Letter from Bonnie

Dad,

My feelings toward you are unexplainable. I can't forgive you for the abuse you did to me. It's hard to tell what I'm going to be like from one day to the next. Yesterday I was really angry, today I'm sad and depressed. I would like to know day to day that I am going to have a positive attitude, but it doesn't always work that way because of you and what you did.

When you abused me, I was wishing I could get away. But no. I couldn't, because you kept me from going and you just kept hitting me. I got so many bruises and they hurt.

At times I wish you were dead, but then I wouldn't have a father; then I would be more depressed than I am now which is really sick.

I've been hurt bad.

Bonnie.

During the first family session, Bonnie spoke from the heart, telling her parents how hurt she was. Luckily, they didn't become defensive (a common reaction). Instead, her father cried. He then revealed that he had been physically abused as a child. Later in the session, he revealed that his violent reactions were due to his intense fear that Bonnie would be raped or kidnapped someday if she failed to heed his warnings about curfews and about where she was allowed to go in her free time.

Bonnie's stepmother also had a history of abuse. Though she cried intensely during the session, she couldn't talk about it. Still, like Bonnie's letter, the session was a good place to start.

Although Bonnie continued to have trouble with her anger, she made considerable progress. Together we worked on her anger toward her biological mother who had abandoned her when she was two. At first, Bonnie felt so hurt she couldn't even write her mother a letter. So we did some meditation. After learning and practicing the technique called Loving Kindness, Bonnie felt that her anger was a lot less troubling, and she was able to talk about her hurt. "I feel very hurt about what my mother did," she said sadly. "I feel like my stepmother is going to walk out on me because that's what all the women in my life have done. I feel like I'm always going to be in trouble, no matter what I do."

Finally, Bonnie was able to write down her feelings in a letter. She wrote about her feelings in the same honest and direct way that she had spoken about them with me.

Like Sally, Bonnie regained her self-esteem through a series of small steps:

- Writing a letter to her father
- Confronting her father with her hurt
- Meditation
- Talking to me about her feelings concerning her biological mother, and her fear of abandonment by her stepmother

- Talking to her parents about her fears

As with Sally, another success story. And it all started with a letter.

Robin's Story

I'm going to say less about Robin's background, because I think her writing speaks so eloquently for itself. I'll share with you two different kinds of writing, to show you how flexible writing as therapy can be.

In brief: Robin was a young woman who had let herself get close to a male friend. He then raped her on a date. It was a cruel blow to her deepest sense of self, but Robin had the guts to take a stand against her pain and loss. She turned to writing as a way to get through it.

Here is a letter Robin wrote, and then a poem. The letter blasts through her anger in a very direct way. It's earthy, blunt, and forceful. For Robin, it was an important step in confronting her feelings without having to confront her perpetrator. (She didn't mail the letter. She didn't have to; by the time she'd finished writing it, it had already served its purpose.)

Then there's her poem. I rejoice in Robin's poem because of her courage, and the tone of quiet victory at the poem's end, that no matter what struggles she must endure ultimately, she will not be a victim.

Robin will free herself from the tie to "the monster on her shoulder."

A Letter from Robin

How dare you talk to me, or even come near me. You are the coldest, meanest asshole. I HATE YOU! You think you are invincible. How dare you treat me like a piece of shit! You deserve to be killed and I wish I could do it. I hope you get so hurt because you will never know how much or in what way you hurt me. But what goes around, comes around, and you better hope I'm not there when you get yours. Because you won't want to live.

Note: Robin's burst of rage through writing was extremely helpful to her and a way to begin her recovery. It is important to know the difference between writing the worst messages imaginable to an abuser and considering acting on it.

Robin's Poem

I sit looking out my window
absorbing the smells and sights of the new
season but all that comes to mind are the
memories and pain of the last time
I saw the changing of this season

It's strange to me how one person

can violate you, change you,
and make you such a part of them
always

I wish nothing more than to forget,
to move on, and to be happy
but the string that binds us is not yet
torn

I know there is a silent struggle we fight
every morning, every afternoon, and
all evenings, a fight I long to win,
a battle that is more important to me than
ANYTHING but I'm unaware of what weapons
to use or how to attack

You appear to me as a strong monster
that cannot be phased
I remember you as a scared boy,
a boy I used to love.
Yet you have become my friend, my enemy,
and my greatest nightmare

Someday I think memories will turn to lessons
and pain to strength,
but what will become of you and that
small string that binds us together

Will you sit as the winter turns to spring
and remember me always, year after year . . .

Will you ever feel the pain
you have inflicted on me

You have changed me, made me,
you are such a part of me
yet you still won't let go

I see you in passing
and try to be the person I once was
but instead, I feel your eyes and
your strength, and I have become
what you have made me to be

My battle will never end
and that string remains . . .
But some day that very string
and this very battle
will destroy you
with everything you are made of

I will sit as the seasons change
and remember your face and hear your name
but I will no longer wonder what your plan is
or what weapon you will choose to use
because I will know
that you can no longer fight a war that does
not exist.

35

Writing Exercises

Writing Exercise #1
Describing your Monster

Step 1. Complete the following sentences:

The monster on my shoulder:
looks like _____
_____
_____

tells me I am_____
_____
_____
_____

makes me feel_____
_____
_____
_____

gives me _____

_____

_____

_____

reminds me of _____

_____

_____

_____

Step 2. Do other things occur to you about your monster? If so, take a piece of paper and begin to "free write." That is, write down any images, ideas, thoughts, statements, or wishes that come to mind. Don't censor anything, and don't worry about grammar, correctness, or spelling. You don't even need to write in complete sentences if you don't want to. The important thing is to freely jot down your thoughts and feelings.

When you are finished, reread what you have written. Do you see any patterns emerging? Does anything surprise you about what you have written?

You can use this exercise whenever you feel the need to understand what your monster is telling you. Over time you may see patterns in the things your monster is saying. Or the monster may change from day to day, experience to experience. This exercise can become the beginning of a journal you keep for yourself. Or you can use these free-write exercises as a way to enhance the process of therapy, giving you and your therapist useful insights into the monsters on your shoulder.

Writing Exercise #2
Talking Back to Your Monster

Step 1. Imagine you are in a quiet room with soft lighting. You are sitting in a chair across from your monster. You are protected from it by an invisible force field, so it cannot hurt you.

What would you like to say to it? Imagine yourself looking right into your monster's eyes.

Jot down a few notes here.

_____

_____

_____

_____

_____

Step 2. Now say these things out loud. Talk to the monster as if it were your perpetrator. Pretend it's actually in the room with you right now. Feel free to say anything and everything that's on your mind.

You may wish to record yourself on a tape recorder so you can play the tape back when you feel you're in a crisis or when you need to talk back to your monster. You can pop the cassette in your car's tape deck (if you have one) so that while driving you can learn and reinforce this self-talk.

Writing Exercise #3
Writing a Letter

Writing a letter to your perpetrator, knowing that you will not mail the letter, is a very powerful tool in the recovery process. It's a good place to begin exploring the power of letter writing as a way of healing. You can use this method whenever you feel the need to voice your feelings directly to your abuser. Or you can address the letter to someone else who has influenced you or who is important in your present-day recovery.

Writing a letter is something you have control over.

The primary goal of this exercise is to help you recall past events. With greater recall will come greater emotion. Although pain inevitably comes with the emotional upsurge, eventually the pain passes and, when it does, hopefully you will feel stronger and clearer.

Writing a letter is something you have control over. You do not need your perpetrator there to help you with this process. (That would be the case if you appealed to your abuser for an apology, or if you actually mailed the letter.) The intention is to voice your feelings directly to the abuser, as if you were talking to him or her right now, without having to go through the trauma of an actual confrontation. Your strength grows from your ability to learn to organize and formalize your feelings of loss and anger. Your feelings of independence will grow, too. Once you begin to write down these feelings and memories in private, you will be better able to begin expressing your loss verbally to a therapist, friend, or loved one.

There are no rules as to what goes into the letter. It helps to write on blank, unlined paper and to handwrite it. For many people, intense emotion is more likely to be released this way. Also, I've found that a lot can be learned from the way a person writes. I'm not an expert in handwriting analysis, but I have come to appreciate handwriting as another window into a person's state of mind. The slant, the intensity of the writing, the use of borders, and other visual clues can be very revealing. If you save your writings and reread them months from now, you may gain new insights into your state of mind.

However, I know some people love using typewriters or word processors, so if that works better for you, go with it.

Most people find the hardest part is just getting started. Sometimes you can feel so powerless that you can't even begin to write a letter to the person who harmed you. Be careful about expecting too much of yourself at the beginning. Some survivors feel that anything short of a magnificent, 20-page essay will be a failure. Keep in mind that this isn't like school; you're doing this just for yourself.

If you feel you can't write anything at all, break the process down into very small steps. Just thinking about what you'd write in a letter might be an easy first step.

The second step could be to actually pen a few brief thoughts or images that flash through your mind. If a paragraph seems like too much to take on, try jotting down a sentence, a phrase, or even just a word. One word can sometimes say more than a thousand words, if it's a word that comes from the heart. And often, when one word is down on the page, it becomes easier to add another and another. That simple step may help break the mental barrier, and the words may start to flow more freely.

What do you do if you just cannot begin to write, no matter how motivated you are? Consider asking someone else to start the letter for you. Working with victims who have a very difficult time starting this process, I've found that I can often help them get started by beginning the letter for them. I generally take an assertive tone. Sometimes I dive right into a hostile tone, just for the impact. Swear words often bring laughter and smiles. As patients hear me voice some of their feelings, they begin to feel freer.

At some point I ask the patients if they can add a word or finish a sentence while I write it down for them. They dictate the letter to me while I write down their words. Next, I encourage them to take the pen and finish the letter themselves. They usually take over from here and do a great job.

You don't have to work with a therapist to do this. A friend or family member could be your writing partner. The key is that both you and the other person must believe in this method and be persistent. Remember, the goal is to break the process down into small, manageable steps.

What do you do once the letter is written? You have many choices. I encourage putting the letter away for a day or two, and then looking at it again. Everything about the way the letter is written provides opportunities for developing greater awareness as to how the abuse has affected the way you think and communicate.

For example, the letter may begin with the word "Dear." Think about what it means to say "dear" to a person who molested, beat, or verbally humiliated you. How do you feel about using this word? It may seem picky to analyze a word like this, but you'd be amazed at how much you can learn by pausing to think about the words you choose, and what they mean to you. Taking another look at your writing, after the first flush of emotion is over, can help you learn about how you may have used language to confuse yourself and deny your pain.

By the way, if you try this step, feel free to re-write the letter any way you please. This is a wonderful way to affirm your growing assertiveness. It gives you visible proof that you CAN be more assertive, that you CAN say "no" to abuse, that you know who the monster is, and it isn't you!

Reading the letter to someone else can also be helpful. This works whether you read your first draft or a later revision. You can ask a friend or relative to listen to you as you read the letter out loud, or you can ask the other person to read it out loud for you. The choice is yours.

> **R**eading the letter to someone else can also be helpful.

If you ask someone else to read the letter first, realize that this step is not the final goal. Eventually, it will be more therapeutic for you to read the letter out loud yourself to someone else. Take your time. Getting a friend to read such a letter is only a step away from being able to read it out loud yourself. Be patient with yourself, and let it happen in its own time.

Once you have written a few letters, the process becomes self-reinforcing. You might collect the letters in a binder as a record of your path in recovery, or you might decide you don't need to save them at all.

Here are some suggestions for other kinds of letters you can create:

- A letter to the nonabusive parent, who may not have helped you as much as you would have liked while the abuse was going on, or who seemed not to know about the abuse

- A letter to a sibling who never knew you were abused (or one who did know, but didn't help you)

- A letter to a friend

- A letter to yourself as a child. (Can you imagine yourself as a loving friend to yourself as a little girl or little boy? What would you, as a caring and compassionate friend, have said to that child?)

- A letter to the "monster(s)" on your shoulder. You can use the notes from Exercises #1 and #2 as a "rough draft" for your letter.

Writing Exercise #4
Telling Your Story

Every person and every family has a story. Sometimes the story, or myth, is happy: a family invents itself as a loving, caring circle. Sometimes a family creates a story about itself that sticks forever, like a gluey monster, like "The Blob" from the famous 1950s movie.

Families can be pulled under by the stories and myths they tell themselves.

Families can be pulled under by the stories and myths they tell themselves: "Dad can't help it; he just needs alcohol to feel good." "We just don't know how to get along as a family. We never have and we never will." "There's no way we can stick together through all this pain." "Mother never loved us."

Like you, my life has had many clear, memorable episodes of joy and pain; dramatic and unexpected events; and interesting and memorable characters who sometimes made me very happy and sometimes made me miserable. The lights and shadows are different for you than for me, but the patterns are probably very similar.

Have you ever thought of your life in this way? As a story, with a shape and structure like a drama?

Sometimes approaching your life as an objective outsider can be an effective way to get a new perspective on what happened to you. One of the things that therapy, and recovery in general, allows you to do is to reinvent the story of your life.

Again, the goal is not to win literary awards or impress anyone with your writing style. You are the author of your own life. It doesn't matter if you make grammatical or spelling mistakes.

In this exercise you will write the story of your life as you have lived it so far. Here are some ideas for stories you can write:

- An episode in your life that made you feel very happy. (You can reread this when you feel down or depressed.)

- An episode in your life that was very painful. (Go slow with this one.)

- The story of your parents' marriage. (Can you think of your parents' lives as two stories that came together? What was the "moral" of this story?)

- The story of your childhood. (What is your earliest memory? Is it happy or sad? Who was with you? When did your childhood begin, and when did it end?)

- The story of your abuse. Do this only if you feel ready to tell the story, and don't feel you

181

have to write the whole story all at once. Again, small pieces of the story are fine.

- The story of your monster. Where did this monster come from? How did it grow? Who "fed" it, and with what "food"?

- The story of your life as a "rewrite," that is, your life as it should have gone up to now, as you would like it to have happened. How is it different from what really happened? Which events would you focus on?

- The story of you ten years from now, who and where you'll be as you grow, change, and move forward positively in your life. Envision yourself as the free, loving, happy person you know you can be. How does the story end?

Writing Exercise #5
Creating a Journal

Keeping a journal is a great way to build a continuous record of your thoughts, feelings, desires, fears, and progress.

A couple of years ago, I read an article in INC. magazine, in which a business consultant was interviewed. His expertise was saving businesses that were failing. For a financial share in the company, he would step in and help rebuild the failing business. I was very impressed with a comment that he

"If you can't write it, you can't speak it."

made about the importance of communication in the workplace. He described an executive whom he had met in his travels. This executive was having trouble in face-to-face interactions, trying to explain his ideas to managers and employees. The business consultant advised the executive to write down his ideas first. His point was simple: "If you can't write it, you can't speak it."

When I read this, I suddenly understood why journal writing had proved so useful for the young people in a drug and alcohol recovery program I was working with at the time. These teens and young adults were overwhelmed with so many issues that they couldn't even talk about them. So they were encouraged to write about their feelings and issues in a journal. It really worked. Somehow, in the act of writing, these troubled youths were able to get out some of the painful problems and concerns bottled up inside them. Once they did that, it was easier for them to talk to a counselor or doctor about what was going on.

A journal is special because it can become anything and everything you want it to be. There are no limits and no rules in creating a journal. You can make it all words, your entries written out or inserted as typed pages. You can add illustrations, striking photographs from magazines, inspiring

> **W**henever you start to feel yourself becoming angry, you can use your journal as a "time out."

stories from the newspaper, art that you do yourself (see the next two chapters), or other "found art."

You can write in the journal whenever you feel like it, and in whatever way is most helpful and healing for you. Some people like to create a journal of their dreams only. Others like to record daily events. Still others focus on crisis points, painful episodes, or feelings that they want to understand better. You may find a journal valuable during those times when you need to talk but no one's around to listen, or when you don't want to talk to another person but need to express your feelings. If your monster is jabbering in your ear in a particularly obnoxious way, writing can take you away from it.

Whenever you start to feel yourself becoming angry, you can use your journal as a "time out." You can collect your thoughts and figure out what it is that's making you so angry or upset.

Many people derive great pleasure from buying a binder, notebook, pad, or blank book. A pretty fabric cover or a soft leather one gives a sensual pleasure that can encourage you on your creative journey through recovery. Even a small choice like this is a positive step toward enhancing your ability to shape your own life and to affirm its innate goodness and beauty.

36

Art as Therapy

Art therapy can be very useful for expressing pain when speaking or writing about it seems too difficult or upsetting.

Some experiences are too harsh for words. Some feelings can't be poured into the linear mold of language. Sometimes you feel overwhelmed and experience many emotions at once. In life and in therapy, there can be paradoxes that seem confusing and hard to deal with at first. In these cases, drawing or painting your feelings can be a huge relief.

> In life and in therapy, there can be paradoxes that seem confusing and hard to deal with at first. In these cases, drawing or painting your feelings can be a huge relief.

Most of us are trained in school to believe visual creativity somehow is less valuable than analysis and logic. Only now are we discovering that intelligence is expressed in many different, equally valuable, ways. Art, music, dance, drama all are creative acts of intelligence and power.

Pleasure in color, shape, texture, and form may be something you never felt as a child. Many abuse survivors feel they were robbed of this pleasure. Carefree, playful, joyous feelings may have been partly or completely squelched. A child burdened with father's alcoholism; a gay teen who is bullied at school; a young girl wondering when and where she's going to be molested next; a minority student fighting against racist harassment; a young boy who is terrified of being hit; these traumatic experiences can make a person feel that innocence and youth are lost forever. Such monsters of abuse consume the creative, exploring, joy of discovery that is the essence of being young, alive, and free.

A way for you to give yourself back some of these moments is to engage in artisitic activities. If, at any point, you feel overwhelmed by your feelings, you can stop for a while and rest. If you feel really troubled, talk to a friend or your therapist. It's alright to work at your art in small, manageable steps. You don't have to be perfect. You don't have to meet anyone's expectation of how you should draw or use your creativity. Pushing yourself too hard will only set you back. Indulging in artistic pleasure should be one way you can just let yourself flow and not worry about other people's ideas or wishes.

37

Art Exercises

There are no strict rules about any of the art exercises that follow. Their purpose is simply to provide you with another method for handling, expressing, and understanding your feelings about the past and about the changes you are experiencing.

It's best if you can use construction paper or heavy paper because it's more durable for saving. However, any type of paper will do: notebook paper, xerox paper, yellow legal pads, recycled paper, blank odds and ends, scraps, even a napkin, in a pinch. Many people like drawing with a heavy pencil or piece of charcoal because they can erase and smudge the lines to create different shading effects. Anything goes. If you like using a ball-point pen, marker, or highlighter, that's fine too.

The exercises that follow are meant to spark your imagination and creativity as you explore your inner world. Feel free to invent your own exercises or to embellish the ones presented here.

Art Exercise #1
Drawing Your Monster

Draw a picture of what your monster looks like. (You may have several different monsters you'd like to draw.)

Try to give the monster some features that are as detailed as possible. Do you picture the monster as a vulture or other predatory bird? Or is it more like a snake, a grizzly bear, or fantasy dragon? Does the monster have a beak, wings, or jagged teeth? How does it move? Does it fly, crawl, or writhe? What are the monster's surroundings?

If you did Writing Exercises #1 and #2 in Chapter 35, you can use your notes from those exercises as a beginning.

Art Exercise #2
Drawing You and Your Monster

Draw yourself with your monster. Again, accuracy is not important here. What's important is how you feel about yourself in relation to the thoughts and ideas your monster represents.

Once you've drawn the picture, ask yourself questions about it to understand what the picture is telling you. What kind of monster did you choose? Why that type and not another? What is the relationship in space between you and the monster? Look at your posture and facial expression and those of your monster. What is the monster doing to you? Where are you? Outside or inside?

You can also try different versions of this exercise. For example:

- Draw yourself as a child, teenager, or adult, as you cope with the monsters on your shoulder

- Draw yourself as a patient in therapy, dealing with your monsters

- If you are in group or family therapy, draw everybody in a room together, with their monsters

- Draw the therapist, counselor, or psychiatrist who is trying to help you with your monsters

- Draw a friend or loved one who has helped you get through the rough times with your monsters

If you and your therapist think it is a good idea, you can bring the pictures to a session so that you can further explore what they mean to you.

Art Exercise # 3
Drawing Your Family

For this exercise, you can try drawing a picture of yourself and your family. Don't worry about making it correct. It can be realistic or abstract if you prefer. The aim is to express your feelings.

You might think about this exercise as follows. If you were trying to show someone what you and your family look like, how would you draw yourselves?

Another approach is to think about drawing family members as characters in a myth or story. It's okay to let your imagination soar. For example, if you feel in a fanciful mood, you could draw your parents as characters in a fairy tale. Some women have told me they sometimes feel like Snow White and their mother is the evil Queen. Other popular tales include Cinderella, Jack and the Beanstalk, and Hansel and Gretel.

While you are drawing, just let the feelings and emotions direct you. Don't worry about analyzing the picture.

If you prefer a more realistic approach, you could try drawing a picture of the home in which you grew up or spent a significant part of your life. You could even draw a particular room. While you are drawing, just let the feelings and emotions direct you. Don't worry about analyzing the picture.

When you are finished, you could put the picture away for a while. In a day or two, it might be useful to come back to it and look at it again. Now is the time to be more analytical about it. You could ask yourself questions such as, what does the room look like? Why did I pick that room out of all the others in the house? What is happening in the room? Where am I, and where are the other members of my family? Why did I draw them like that? How do I feel when I look at this picture?

You can show the picture to a friend, family member, or to your therapist, especially if you want to talk about something in the picture or the memories it evokes.

If you do this exercise a number of times over a period of six months or a year, you may find interesting changes in the way you draw and represent yourself in relation to family members.

Art Exercise #4
Drawing the Future

This exercise allows you to visualize yourself in the future. Picture yourself at the end of treatment after healing has occurred. Most of us never quite finish working on our problems, but we may have an idea — an image, or mental picture — of how we will look and how we will feel when we reach a more serene, happy stage of life.

Picture yourself at the end of treatment after healing has occurred.

You are working very hard to recover, to heal, to get on a better path in life. Try imagining yourself walking on a road. The road is your recovery path.

Now try drawing yourself on this road. Think about where you would like to be in two, five, ten, or twenty years from now. What will you look like at each of those stages? Will there be people around you, joining you on this road? Feel free to draw whatever comes to mind.

What do you see along the path? Are there any monsters lurking in the bushes or alongside the road? There may be something at the end of the road, something you are walking toward. What is it? What does it look like?

As an alternative, you could draw your "safe place" that I talked about in Chapter 32 on self-hypnosis. Some people like to draw a picture of how their world would look without their monsters constantly voicing criticism, blame, or rebukes. Perhaps the trees would look a bit greener, the sky bluer, the water clearer and more sparkling. Perhaps you would be walking along with a smile on your face, or plucking a spring flower from the side of the road. Draw whatever you feel like drawing.

Even if the picture doesn't turn out the way you thought it would, you may learn something about your feelings at that moment.

You might start with a rough sketch in pencil or pen. If you like the result, you could do another, more finished drawing, in brightly colored crayons, magic markers, colorful pens, or paints.

Again, there are no rules here. You are in control. It's your picture, and your life! Even if the picture doesn't turn out the way you thought it would, you may learn something about your feelings at that moment. If you don't like the drawing, you can always throw it away and start another. But if the picture makes you feel good, if it supports your vision of the safe place, then you might save it to use before beginning your self-hypnosis exercise. You could even put it on the wall to inspire you and remind you of your own creative, healing vision.

Art Exercise #5
Multi-Media Monsters

In addition to drawing, there are many other wonderful kinds of art forms or media that you can enjoy and use as tools in your beast-busting "toolbox." Here are some suggestions for multi-media activities. If you want to learn more about them, ask your librarian or consult your local bookstore.

Photography

As the saying goes, "a picture is worth a thousand words."

Photography is a powerful medium. As a tool in your recovery, it can be very useful because photographs are another kind of record of the past and present.

Find a picture of yourself that you feel shows the "true you" as a child — that open, innocent person before abuse, trauma, or hurtful awareness.

You might find a picture of yourself that you feel shows the "true you" as a child—that open, innocent person before abuse, trauma, or hurtful awareness. Pin the picture up on the wall, over your desk, or, if you prefer, a more private place, such as your wallet. Only you will know that it's there. This picture might become a kind of "totem" or symbol of the "you" that was lost through abuse. Hold onto it as a reminder that you were a young person full of life and dreams. That is the "real" you. The "you" before the monsters.

Other activities with photography include putting together a photo album of your recovery, in which you take pictures of yourself at various stages over a period of time, such as a year. Putting photos side by side, or one after another, can create a visual record of your progress. They can show you where the ups and downs took place, and can encourage you. It is amazing how sometimes photographs show people changing over time. The light comes back into their eyes, depression lifts from their shoulders, their jaws unclench, they become more physically fit, they wear brighter colors, more flattering clothing, they stand a bit more proudly, and so forth.

If you feel up to it, you could put together an album of your childhood. Sometimes looking at pictures yields new insights into family patterns and relationships. It is interesting to look at the spatial relationships between people in pictures. For example, some people find that when they look at a picture of themselves and their family, they are standing somewhat awkwardly apart from their parents or siblings.

Facial expressions also reveal a lot. The camera has an eerie way of picking up emotions that people may not be aware of or that they are trying to hide.

If you enjoy taking pictures, then using a camera can be a great way to record people, places, and events that are meaningful to you during your healing.

Again, take your time. Only do what you feel like doing, and what will not overwhelm you or flood you with painful feelings too hard to handle right now. These activities are for your benefit only, so it's up to you to decide what pace is right for you.

Painting

Paints, ranging from finger paints to expensive oil paints, are an expressive medium to work in. The colors are so rich and the shades so vibrant. When you paint, you can use the same exercises as for drawing, but employ the rich colors of paints to express your feelings and thoughts in even more vivid, varied ways.

Watercolors appeal to many people because of their softness. The fluid, gentle colors create images that evoke the swirling, loose patterns of the mind. Oil paints are great for creating heavier, thick images on canvas or wood. Since oil paints require more set-up and clean-up, many people prefer to use acrylics which can be diluted and cleaned with water. Oils require turpentine. Use whatever type of paint you enjoy, and feel free to consult your local art store for more suggestions about projects with paint.

Ceramics (clay)

Some people find great pleasure in working with clay. Clay can be molded, pressed, and pounded into any shape you want. Picking up a hunk of clay and pretending it's your monster or your abuser can be a therapeutic way of getting out your anger and rage without hurting anyone or yourself. You can shape the clay to make faces or bodies. You can make a model of your own body at a particular point in time, then change it to show the effects of an event or new understanding. You can create the figure of an animal or beast. The choices are limitless.

You can buy inexpensive modeling clay at any all-purpose store or at an art supply store. It helps if you have a flat, relatively clean surface to work on in a space where you will not damage anything if you throw the clay and work vigorously with it. A garage or basement works for some people as a private art space. Others prefer a small corner of their apartment, or a room in their house where they can create a studio.

Collage

Collage is another great medium because you can use anything—fabric, feathers, paper cups, photographs, drawings, cardboard, paper clips, you name it—to glue onto a canvas or board to create interesting pictures or small-scale models.

You could create a "monster board" on which you glue different objects or items that represent your monster or abuser. Or you could make a "recovery board" of various objects and images to inspire you as you move ahead in therapy or in healing.

38

New Communication Part 1

Just about everyone wants to communicate better. When I give talks or work privately with people, I hear how much they want to communicate better with family members, friends, and people at work. The dilemma is that they don't know how to do it.

Not all of us were lucky enough to have been born into families with healthy communication styles. Many of us had to learn it on our own after failures in our relationships. Negative voices in our heads often interfere with truthfully expressing how we feel in clear, non-threatening ways.

I believe that many sensitive social problems challenge our ability to communicate well. For example, today we have to deal with the issue of substance abuse or sexual activity among children and teens. These can be awkward issues to talk about. They really challenge our methods of communication.

To change the way you communicate, you need to know where you're headed. A new way of communicating you hope to adopt must fit comfortably with who you are and what you stand for, as well as what you want to stand for in the future. Attempting to take on a style of communication that is uncomfortable will only result in failure, causing you to revert to your previous, more familiar style.

I suggest that you identify a style that you think might be right for you. It's helpful to identify an author who speaks or writes the way you'd like to; or a method of communicating that appeals to you and seems to match what you're aiming for. In these four chapters on communication, I will identify and describe methods of communication that many of my patients have found helpful. I have adopted this style myself and find it works well even in discussions of difficult issues. None of these communication methods are new. If you think about the good communicators you know, you'll notice they use these same methods, to varying degrees. However, for some of us, they will appear to be new methods.

This chapter focuses on common communication problems and how to recognize them. Chapters 39-41 offer some solutions to these problems and give you suggestions for enhancing your communication skills.

A word of caution: learning and applying new communication methods is hard work. It takes time and practice. Developing a new attitude about how you measure personal success is the key to your feeling successful. It helps to set your goals in such a way that you can be successful a high percentage of the time. *The best way to do this is to learn to measure success based on your own behavior, not on the behavior of others.*

Ultimately the goal is for you to develop your own personal communication style that empowers you without imposing on the feelings of others.

> Learn to measure success based on your own behavior, not on the behavior of others.

Improving your communication skills will help you feel more confident about your ability to protect yourself and to express your needs. Most people find that this newfound confidence enhances both the recovery process and life in general.

"You" Statements

There's probably no worse way to communicate with another person than to use a "you" statement. "You make me feel . . .," "You never . . .," or "You are . . .," are accusatory comments.

When a sentence is started with "you," it can have the effect of raising the other person's defenses. A "you" statement is generally perceived as a criticism, even if it is not meant that way. When you want to deal with a problem and start off by using the word "you," it's like pointing a finger at the other person. Even worse, it can feel as if you're poking at their chest. When this happens, the other person tends to strike back and a struggle for control begins.

So why do we persist with "you" statements? Often it's just a bad habit, or we're not even aware that we're doing it. Sometimes we believe the other person is at fault and deserves blame. While other times, when we start a discussion like this, we're angry and may not fully realize what we're saying.

Speaking for yourself and opening with an "I feel" statement is much more effective for being heard and creating feelings of empathy in the other person. In Chapter 39, I discuss this positive communication style in greater depth.

Rigid Statements

In addition to using "you" statements, too often we use language in such a way that we box ourselves into a corner. You can inadvertently set yourself up for control struggles with others, struggles that you will never win. You can place such high expectations on yourself that you are almost guaranteed to feel like a failure.

How do you do this? By using words such as "should," "must," "can't," "won't," "have to," and "got to." There are many other similar expressions, all of them sounding like restrictions and negative judgments. A sneaky one is "enough," as in, "good enough" or "smart enough." These words or phrases can set you and the other person up for black and white thinking. Such words create the effect that, in order to be successful, you or the other person must do something in only one way, manner or style. There is no room for imperfection or for individual differences in personality or approach. It's all or nothing.

The best way to get out of this pattern is to learn to substitute a more compassionate statement, such as "I think it would be better . . .," or "I suggest that . . .," or even, "I would prefer that" (if you are expressing your own wishes). Saying "I think you would do better . . ." is a more effective way of reaching someone. It's a suggestion with no strings attached, no expectations, and no demands. When you talk this way, you are expressing your own view and the other person is free to make up his or her own mind, to agree or disagree.

Triangulation

Triangulation is a concept that I think can be intimidating to many people, but it's really very simple. I touched on triangulation in Chapter 12, "Take a Message," but I'd like to go into further detail here to help you understand the concept fully.

Triangulation means talking about a problem with just about anyone except the person you're having difficulty with. It often feels safer to speak to a go-between than to deal directly with the person and risk conflict.

Think of a triangle and its three sides. Instead of a relationship between two points, triangulation fosters a confusing connection among all three. Triangulation is very common. We do it so often that we think it is normal. A form of triangulation

It often feels safer to speak to a go-between than to deal directly with the person and risk conflict.

is "gossip." We talk behind people's backs to alleviate our anger, frustration, and fear of dealing directly with the person. Then we feel relief that we have avoided trouble.

Here's a typical example: Mother and Father are having marital problems, but they aren't talking to each other about it. Instead, Mom talks to her daughter. She feels better as a result of confiding her problems in someone else. The short-term effect is positive for Mom. She feels less anxiety. However, the daughter starts to feel weighed down by the monster of knowledge of her parents' conflicts. A triangle is starting to emerge, with the two parents and the daughter each occupying a point. The monster moves from shoulder to shoulder. It may have started on Dad's shoulder, leaped over to Mom's by way of an abusive remark, and then onto the daughter's shoulder as a nervous comment. Each step reduces anxiety until the monster lands on the next person's shoulder.

The triangulation can take different forms at this point. First, the daughter can simply serve as a confidante for the mother and nothing more. The monster in this situation often feels very flattering. For example, the mother might say to her daughter, "Nobody else understands me the way you do." Or, "You understand me better than your father." This monster-talk may relieve the mother's tension, but it damages the daughter's relationship with her father. It also hurts the parents' relationship with each other because it creates emotional distance between them through distrust and a breach of their confidence in one another.

It can get even worse. The daughter can serve as a go-between. Now she informs Father what Mother is feeling. Father's anger at Mother can be directed at the daughter, the messenger. This is an unhealthy role for the daughter. People have a tendency to play "Kill the Messenger" when they hear things they don't like (see Chapter 12).

Another way of looking at this experience is that the father now gets to take aim at an offensive monster. He probably won't like what his daughter tells him, and most likely he'll lash out. The problem is that the monster has hitched a ride on an innocent person's shoulders. The daughter is the one who'll receive the tongue-lashing. This process is especially outrageous because the monster could have been Dad's monster to begin with. Regardless of where the problem originates, the fighting back and forth via the daughter makes her the innocent victim.

Why do triangles occur so often? Because in the short-term, people generally feel better when they "Dump the monster" onto someone else, bringing a relief of tension and avoiding a feared confrontation with the actual target of bad feelings. In the long run, however, this method of communicating is counter productive. It doesn't solve the problem. It creates additional problems.

This relates to the business world as well. For example, there's a saying in the sales profession that, on average, an angry customer will tell 25 people about his dissatisfaction. He'll tell everyone but the salesperson himself! That's a lot of negative publicity, and it's due to triangulation. If the salesperson could learn to identify when someone is angry or displeased and then get the customer to talk about it, the negative publicity would stop.

Although they do not use the word triangulation, authors Blanchard, Oncken, and Burrows in their book, *The One Minute Manager Meets the Monkey*, discuss interesting work they've done on a similar subject in the business world. (See the Resources section.) These authors use a monkey image to describe the process when managers mistakenly take responsibility for problems that don't belong to them. It's a clever way to talk about a kind of miscommunication that comes very close to triangulation. In both cases, the responsibility for the problem is taken on by the wrong person.

In my view, triangulation is very similar to an addictive process. Persons who are physically addicted to drugs often use the drug to relieve great inner anxiety or tension. They take the drug and the feeling of anxiety goes away for a while. This is similar to the first feelings of relief experienced when triangulation occurs. But then the drug addict needs more of the substance to feel better. It's a never-ending and quite vicious circle of dependency. Similarly, in a family where triangulation is the main method of communication, people have a hard time getting out of that style. It becomes so comfortable to avoid direct confrontations that the family needs more and more indirect communication just to maintain the balance of power.

How can you break this pattern of addiction? I suggest a two-fold process.

First, the cycle must be broken. The pattern must be interrupted so a new one can emerge.

Second, healthier ways of communicating must be learned and practiced.

The most effective way to break out of an addictive pattern is to go "cold turkey." Stop altogether. The symptoms will get worse for a while, but eventually disappear, and a much healthier "organism" will develop.

At first it will seem very uncomfortable not to use that way of talking and relating. Problems between people may seem to grow worse as new tensions arise and more direct confrontations lead to strain. I often advise children, for example, simply to refuse to accept "the monster" from their parents. The daughter might tell Mom not to talk to her but directly to Dad about their marital problems. Mom probably won't like to hear this, and Dad may not want to hear what Mom has to say.

However, if they stick with it, healthier, more direct, and more positive ways of communicating will become familiar to them. The same is true for you. If you practice better ways of communicating, ultimately you will find they work so much better than the old way that you won't want to go back.

The next three chapters explore some of these positive skills.

39

New Communication Part 2

Now I'd like to talk about some of the positive ways you can communicate in order to improve your relationships with yourself and others.

Self-Talk

One area that is often overlooked is the sphere of self-talk or self-communication. I think focusing on how we talk to ourselves is the ideal place to begin learning a new communication style. If people are particularly harsh or abrasive in their communication style with others, they are usually speaking that way to themselves in their private thoughts.

Underneath poor communication styles is often an unfriendly monster from your past that is saying very negative things to you. This "monster-talk" can set you up to be easily demoralized or irritated. Most of the time, the monsters are not yours; instead, they were given to you by someone in your past. The beastly voices are a holdover from your relationship with that person.

Frequently criticizing yourself with harsh and painful comments such as "you're stupid" or "what a jerk" can be very harmful. Instead, you can learn new ways of talking to yourself that encourage tolerance, respect, and empathy. You can learn to speak to yourself as someone who doesn't have to be perfect all the time. When you catch yourself using statements like "I should have . . .," "I have to . . ." or "Why can't I ever . . ." (comments which

> **Y**ou can learn to speak to yourself as someone who doesn't have to be perfect all the time.

leave no room for growth, change, or human foibles), try changing the way you talk to yourself.

Beware of the monster-talk and learn to identify how it is affecting you. (I hope that stories in Part 2 of this book have helped you do some of that work already.) As you learn to identify and reject these abusive monsters, you will develop more supportive types of self-talk.

Begin to include statements like, "I think I would do better if . . .," or "That's not how I usually . . .," or "Maybe next time I can . . . ." These have a very different tone from the first set of phrases. The harshness and rigidity are gone. So is the "all-or-nothing" quality. You can make mistakes, and you can grow; you don't have to get it right all the time.

Learning a new style of "self-talk" not only will improve your feelings about yourself, but will also improve the way you talk to and relate to others. I think that it is very hard for us to learn to communicate better with others before we learn how to communicate better with ourselves. Our outer style reflects our inner style. So as you read the other positive communication tips in the following pages, keep in mind that you can also apply them to the way you talk to yourself.

Avoiding Control Struggles

Too often we find ourselves involved in control struggles with other people. We set ourselves up for these conflicts when we measure our personal success by how others react or behave. Clear, effective communication happens when we free ourselves from these harmful control struggles and learn to put the locus of approval in our own hearts and minds.

If I approach an interaction with another person with the need to have them agree with me, apologize, accept blame, praise me, and so forth, then I am setting myself up for a control struggle. If I need someone to react in a certain way so that I can feel good about myself, then the potential for a control struggle exists and it will probably occur.

When the struggle starts, it usually leads to anger, tension, and arguments over who's right and who's wrong.

To take this issue to an extreme, I think that the ultimate insult and humiliation for abuse victims occurs when they reproach themselves for failing to get some kind of response from their abuser. People often set themselves up for this by building up their courage to confront the abuser but then backing down when the abuser denies responsibility, refuses to apologize, or lashes out. The victim winds up feeling like a failure. That's an extreme example, but it shows how deadly it can be to put the responsibility for how you feel about yourself onto another person.

The same idea applies to most breakdowns in communication. If you learn to measure your personal success by what YOU say and do rather than by what others say and do, then you will find you are not sparking control struggles with others, and communication will be much easier and more amiable.

40

New Communication Part 3

In this chapter and the next, I'd like to focus on some specific methods for enhancing positive communica tion with others. You might think of the theme of this chapter as "accentuate the positive," and the next as, "eliminate the negative," like in the familiar song lyric.

"I Feel" Statements

As I mentioned earlier, using "I feel" statements is a powerful way of taking responsibility for your role in a dialogue. When you talk this way, you reduce the likelihood of a control struggle. For example, when you say "I feel hurt" or "I feel sad," no one can disagree with that. It's your feeling. You own it. You're not putting your feelings or judgments onto somebody else.

If someone then engages you in a control struggle about what you've said, they will be showing you to what lengths they are willing to go to deny your feelings and concerns. If someone does that, you'll be able to respond confidently, with "I merely stated my feelings. I own my feelings. I said nothing about you or how you should feel. So why are we arguing?"

Once you've mastered the "I feel" statement and come to appreciate its value, you will be better able to see that control struggles develop mainly because language is used inappropriately. Language was not intended to be divisive. It was developed to bring people together. It was meant to be a bridge, not a barrier.

> **C**ontrol struggles develop mainly because language is used inappropriately.

I know it can be difficult to use this technique when you are really upset with someone. An "I feel" statement can sound so trite and silly to your own ears sometimes. But it is the most effective way to express your needs as a way to ask someone else to change their behavior.

I have seen living proof of this in my own life. Let me share another story with you.

The value of "I feel" statements was once driven home to me when I witnessed an interaction between my son and his friend. At the time, Ben was about 6½, and Adam was 4½. I was driving them, along with Adam's best friend Barry, to the beach.

Shortly after Barry got into the car, he suddenly blurted out that my older son, Ben, was his "best friend." I looked at Adam's face and saw instant pain and disappointment. After all, Barry was supposed to be his best friend. Adam became very quiet and just gazed straight ahead.

I felt I needed to do something. But what?

My first instinct was to try to get Barry to apologize. But I knew that would be useless, and I didn't like the idea of solving Adam's problem for him (especially when I wasn't exactly sure what to do!). I wondered whether one of Barry's "monsters on the shoulder" might not be lurking behind his comment. But I really wasn't sure. So I decided to practice what I preach in my office and encourage Adam to use an "I feel" statement.

I suggested to Adam that he tell Barry how he was feeling. At first, Adam didn't say anything. Then I urged him to try saying, "Barry, I feel hurt." So Adam turned to Barry and said, "That hurts me, Barry." I breathed a sigh of relief, hoping that I had done something to help my son.

But a moment later, Barry repeated that Ben was his best friend.

Again I felt Adam's pain, and again I encouraged him to tell Barry how he was feeling.

So Adam said, "Barry, I feel hurt when you say that." Barry looked out the window for a moment. Then, to my surprise, he turned to Adam and said, "Ben likes you better than he likes me."

Something clicked at that point, something I hadn't realized before. I looked at Barry and said, "Barry, does that mean that the reason you said Ben was your best friend was because you want him to like you more?" Barry said yes. I then explained how Barry's first statement, which had felt to Adam like a put-down, was really a compliment to Adam. Barry had seen that Ben really liked Adam, and that had made him feel left out.

As we talked, Adam realized that Barry was really pointing out something positive about him: that his older brother really liked him. What had at first seemed like a rejection turned out to be a kind of admiration, even envy for how much Adam was cared for.

Adam was delighted. I could see that the monster of rejection had been lifted off his shoulders. When we got to the beach, we all had a great time together. I felt especially relieved because I actually had done all right in this situation, even though I had started out not knowing what to do. I had placed my faith in the power of "I feel" statements as a way out of hurt and denial. And it worked.

"I feel" statements are simple; you don't have to learn a lot of psychological jargon to use them, though it does take some time before they feel comfortable. The key is to have faith. In the above example, it took three tries before the real reason behind the apparent "insult" emerged.

So persist with the "I feel" statement as long as it takes. Stay with how you feel, and sooner or later you'll find a communication bridge to the other person. It's a good way to keep the monsters from creeping in and coming between you and the people you care about.

Positive Reinforcement

Using "I feel" statements can do a great deal to improve your communications with others, but you can also shape other people's behavior by letting them know how you would like to be treated in the future. The best way to do this is to focus on and reinforce the positive things they do, rather than harping on their negative qualities or actions.

It's been proven in research that acknowledging behavior in a warm, positive way known as "positive reinforcement" is much more likely to lead to behavior change than negative responses like criticism, blame, nagging, or yelling. Just as talking negatively tends to yield a negative response, sending positive messages tends to bring you positive reactions tenfold.

People like to be affirmed; it feels good to be appreciated and admired. Compliments—if they are sincere, not forced or phony—express your appreciation of the other person. Giving praise and compliments to others sends a message that you notice the good things about them. This invites them to do the same toward you. So you subtly shape their behavior even when there isn't a problem between you that needs to be dealt with.

You can use this technique in all types of communications. It can work for you as a good way to maintain an even keel in a relationship, a kind of "protective maintenance" to keep good feelings humming along. It can work with co-workers, associates, friends, and family members. People tend to flower under nice words and congenial talk, as long as the words are sincerely meant.

The best way to do this is to identify something truly positive about the other person. Then let the person know how much you appreciate that quality. There are many genuinely positive things about most people that can be identified if we just take the time to look.

This technique also works at times when you need to convey that you don't like what someone did, when you wish to convey that you want them to behave differently in the future.

For example, if someone is rude, the knee-jerk negative reaction would be to say something like, "What a stupid, thoughtless thing to say. I can't believe you could be so rude." That kind of put-down is only likely to yield an equally defensive response from the other person.

Instead, try using a little positive reinforcement, like the comments suggested by Blanchard and Johnson in *The One Minute Manager* (see Resources). For example, you can say "I feel hurt," followed by "especially because you're one of the most considerate people I know." Or you could say, "I know that you can be very thoughtful and sensitive, so what you just said surprises me. Can we talk about it?" Or you could say, "I know you didn't mean to hurt my feelings just now, but I felt hurt by what you said. It took me by surprise, because you've always been so considerate to me."

These statements open up the issue in a direct but nonthreatening way. The other person is less likely to get defensive if you approach the issue by showing that both you and the other person deserve respect.

The general idea behind this type of communication is that you first let the person know how you feel, using nonoffensive "I feel" statements, and then you follow up with a compliment which actually shapes the other person's behavior in a more positive direction. Positive reinforcement lets people know how you like to be treated, and it does this in a constructive way.

Zig Ziglar, the motivational speaker and sales trainer, has a wonderful metaphor that I'd like to share with you. He says, "When you're digging a gold mine, you don't dig for dirt. You dig for gold."

In a nutshell, that's what positive reinforcement means. You don't look for the "dirt" and try to dig out another person's monsters. You look for the gold. Believe that the gold is there, find it, and then reward it.

I am not encouraging phony recognition or a Pollyanna approach to life. Many situations are complex and require persistent, patient effort before they can be resolved. There's no one perfect way to communicate, and sometimes even our best efforts to talk positively seem to fall on deaf ears. But effective communicators are constantly digging for "gold," accentuating the positive, in themselves as well as in others.

It's a never-ending process, but it's well worth it.

41

New Communication Part 4

You may be thinking, okay, all these ideas for better communication are great, and I'll try them starting today. But what do you do when you just get so angry that you feel as if you're going to explode? What about when someone annoys you so much or disappoints you so deeply that you can't say anything good at all? What do you do when you feel rage?

In angry situations, people's monsters tend to go into overdrive.

That's what this chapter is all about: how to defuse tense or negative situations in which you feel that positive communication seems impossible. In other words, how to "eliminate the negative."

Many times I have seen people try to communicate when one or the other is very angry; often it simply doesn't work. In angry situations, people's monsters tend to go into overdrive. Our irrational fears and irritations, or our rightful grievances, fuel our monsters' rage and push us to hasty judgments and reprisals. Our voices take on an edge of "do-or-die," "win or lose." Once the battle lines are drawn, we're boxed in and we can't back down.

It doesn't have to be this way. There are a number of things you can do to give both you and the other person an "out."

Learn to Wait

When emotions are hot and feelings are running high, it's useful to take a break. It's the "time out" principle used with kids, but it works with adults too. Try taking a coffee break, a bathroom break, or a break for a drink of water. No matter how angry you are, this gesture can prove very effective. Just when the person is expecting more hostility, you act in a neutral way.

Here's a personal example to show you what I mean. When I was in residency training as a psychiatrist, I had a patient who was very difficult to deal with. When my supervisor listened to an audiotape of the session, she pointed out I had completely derailed the session by allowing myself to get angry at the patient. I wasn't aware that I had done this, but when she replayed the tape, I realized what she was talking about.

I then asked my supervisor for suggestions about what to do when I felt angry at a patient. She suggested that I take a coffee break or bathroom break. Just then, I realized she had been taking several breaks during the session with me; apparently she'd been feeling angry at me, but instead of "letting me have it" she took a "time out" and collected her thoughts. From my point of view as her student, this technique was a godsend. It had allowed her to keep her cool and get her points across without becoming openly hostile.

Many times if you take a break you'll find that this also gives the other person a chance to do the same. Here's another example from my relationship with my residency supervisor. During one supervisory session, she was rude and hostile toward me from the start of the meeting. I didn't think I had done anything to deserve such treatment.

We both took a short break. When we returned, I told her how I felt. All I said was, "I feel hurt, and I don't see what I've done to deserve being treated like this." She quickly told me I was absolutely right, and then explained that right before our session she had fired her secretary. It turned out the secretary had deleted an entire manuscript from the computer, and since academics live and die by what they publish, this was a disaster. I told her I understood how she could be so upset. Then she apologized for the way she'd behaved toward me, and the rest of the supervisory session was great.

See how it works? We'd both cooled off a bit, and since she was basically a very thoughtful and reasonable person, she'd had a chance to think about what was going on. I'd also had a chance to think about what I was going to say, and how I was going to say it. In a sense, we both took responsibility for our roles in the dialogue.

This leads us to another reason why breaks are helpful: it gives you a chance to think about your timing.

Right now, today, or even this week, might not be the best time to let someone know how you feel. If you value the message you're trying to communicate, then you may wish to put off talking about your concerns until the person is better able to hear you, or until you are more in command of your feelings and intentions. When you sense that you and the other person are in a better frame of mind, then you can resume the discussion by asking permission to talk about what occurred.

For example, you can resume the dialogue by saying, "When we spoke the last time, I felt there was a great deal of tension. I think it would be helpful to discuss what happened. Do you mind?"

In this message, you state your feeling, own the feeling, identify a need, and request a discussion. This helps avoid a control struggle. There's no risk of failure; you're not giving the other person control over your thoughts and feelings. If the other person says no, you're still a success. You showed a willingness to continue the dialogue in a healthy and open manner. If the other person says yes, you're more likely to get a better response to your concerns than when everyone's emotions were running high.

Another technique that can work is to let others interrupt you when you sense they have something urgent to say. In many situations, this strategy can really help. Why? Because when people want very much to interrupt you, it means that at that moment they are no longer listening to you. They are concentrating on, and anxious to get you to hear, what they want to say. They're not hearing your words, no matter how loudly you try to shout them down. They're focused on how to get your attention and how to convince you that they are right. In other words, they are enmeshed in a control struggle with you. The monsters on their shoulders, the need to be dominant, in this case, have taken over.

The best posture in that kind of moment is to not join the struggle. It's a waste of time. Yelling back and forth won't solve anything. So instead, stop talking and encourage the person to say what's on his mind. Try not to take the interruption personally. Once the other person has had his full say, he'll probably be in a better frame of mind to hear what you have to say. You'll probably find the give-and-take is back in the conversation.

Write It Down

This technique works nicely if you can take a quick break, but it also can help even if you can't. Jotting down a few notes about why you are getting so angry lets you sort through your emotions. Even if you only scribble a few random associations on a pad while someone is talking to you, it can help break the vicious cycle of rising tempers. It can free you to spot some of your own monsters that may be lurking in the wings.

For example, one day when a friend was talking to me about a personal problem, I realized that I was becoming angry. I was listening to my friend but at the same time I could feel my blood pressure rising. We were sitting at my kitchen table, so I quickly grabbed a little notepad for taking phone messages and just jotted down a few words that came to mind. A few moments later I glanced down at the pad. I was surprised to see that I had written the following: "Nothing is working. He's not listening to my ideas. He's my friend and I should be able to help him."

In a flash I realized why I was getting so angry. It was because I felt like nothing I had been saying was helping him. My "monster" said that because I'm a doctor I should have the answers to everything. By "free-writing" I had tapped into my own perfectionism. I saw that this monster was getting in the way of what was really needed here. My friend didn't need me to solve his problem; he just wanted to talk and release his feelings. At that point I just leaned back and let myself listen. My anger subsided because I wasn't putting pressure on myself to have an instant solution. I tapped into my empathy for my friend, which had always been there, under the "monster-talk."

During longer breaks, for example, if a day or a week goes by before you see the person again, you can write longer pieces such as journal entries or even a letter as if you were going to mail it to the person. They can be helpful in sorting out a more complex range of feelings.

If writing strikes you as a hard thing to do, that's okay. Many of us have "writing phobias" for one reason or another. If you feel nervous about writing, see my discussion of writing as therapy in Chapter 34 and the exercises in Chapter 35. They may be able to help.

Use Humor

Famed humorist Victor Borge says that laughter is the shortest distance between two people.

Humor is a gift. When we tell a joke or a funny story, it's like giving a gift of happiness and pleasure to other people. I enjoy making people laugh. It's a way to help people enjoy the moment to its fullest potential. Even the most tense or awkward situations (perhaps especially these) can be redirected with a gentle dose of humor.

Self-effacing humor is a powerful way of forming bonds and defusing tension. Putting yourself in a position where the joke is on you can be a sign of strength and a gesture which shows you trust your audience. It can help draw you and others closer together, like a healing bridge.

I frequently encourage patients to spend time learning about humor. Many people grew up in homes where humor was not valued as the building block that it is. Also, when people are depressed, they often lose their sense of humor. Abuse victims plunged in a depression may find it harder and harder to remember how it feels to laugh, to have a light-hearted moment. This is especially true when you are recalling memories and experiences that hurt, plain and simple. When this happens, you may go numb to humor altogether. Tapping into the sources of amusement and laughter can be like a "tune-up" that can restore a bit of perspective to a rough time.

I also encourage you to learn about different kinds of humor so that you can refine your awareness of when humor works and when it doesn't. Not all humor is healing. Sarcasm, for example, is often hostility veiled as humor, like a monster wearing a funny party mask. Sarcasm is a way to get someone to smile while you stab them in the back. At the moment, the laughter feels good and seems to draw people closer together. But afterwards, the recipient is often aware that a put-down has landed on his shoulders. The person may feel hurt and angry. When this happens, they'll usually try to get even somehow.

That's why refining your sense of humor can be a good move. The more you know how to use humor well, the better you will be able to inject a little levity into tense moments, or introduce it regularly into your everyday interactions. Listening to standup comedy on audio- or videotapes, or reading funny books by humorists and comedy writers can help jump start "the laughing center" of the brain and keep your sense of humor tuned up.

Use Empathy

One of the most powerful ways to communicate and to avoid control struggles in which each person's monster locks horns is to use empathy.

Empathy means *understanding* what someone else feels. This is different from sympathy, which means *feeling* what someone else feels. The difference is important. Psychotherapy is built around the therapist's empathy for the patient; without empathy, the treatment would be cold and inhuman. However, although the therapist uses his or her imagination and understanding to empathize with the patient, the therapist does not dive right into the feelings along with the suffering person. If a therapist were to feel this kind of sympathy for all his patients at every moment, he or she would quickly burn out.

Empathy strengthens communication because it is another kind of bridge, a bridge of understanding. In angry situations, it's very helpful to try to view things from the other person's point of view. When you have a chance to understand the reasons behind another person's behavior, you will find that there is always an explanation that makes sense to the other person. The reason may not always be rational, but it does exist. And you probably will find that you have nothing whatever to do with the underlying cause.

If you practice this skill often enough, eventually you can learn to accept that there is always a reason. You don't have to know the specific reason in order to share empathy. You just trust that it's there. Once you realize this, you will feel less need to react angrily or defensively.

Often the people who evoke these hostile feelings in you are really in a great deal of pain themselves. They simply are doing their best to survive their own internal chaos and hurt. I have found that it helps to say to myself that they are probably treating themselves one hundred times worse with negative self-talk than they are treating me.

Understanding this basic principle of human nature doesn't mean that you're enjoying the fact that someone else is treating himself in an unloving, sadistic way. It means that you can feel empathic, because you know the other person is struggling with his or her own internal monsters. The nasty wall of words directed at you then becomes like some kind of funny "monster mirror." You can see that the other person is trying to turn you into a monster in order to get a very oppressive beast off his own shoulders.

This kind of insight may be just the pause you need to allow yourself to listen, wait, and then share your own feelings through an "I feel" statement and a compliment or affirmation.

"The Ten Suggestions"

I had a chuckle recently with a friend. We were talking about the terrible impact of all the "shoulds" in our heads, the monsters of expectations, perfectionism, criticism, and blame. I happen to be Jewish, so that's my frame of reference. I was musing about the Ten Commandments with my friend, when I began playfully thinking about the words. "I wonder what our lives would be like," I said, "if instead of the Ten Commandments, we had been given the Ten Suggestions." That's thinking like a psychiatrist, right? But seriously, I like to think of suggestions as a better kind of self-talk and communication style, for all the reasons I've given in the last few chapters.

So, to practice what I preach about using humor, here's a wrap-up of "The Ten Suggestions" for better communication.

The Ten Suggestions

1. Use "I feel" statements.
2. Avoid rigid language.
3. Be direct; avoid triangulation.
4. Use positive self-talk.
5. Stay out of control struggles.
6. Use positive reinforcement.
7. Learn to wait (take a break).
8. Write it down.
9. Use humor.
10. Use empathy.

With these 10 "suggestions" you can greatly enhance how you relate to people in your life, as well as influence how you will be treated in return. You will be better able to avoid conflicts and frustration. You will have a stronger base from which to strive for an open, honest, and nonabusive relationship.

At first it may seem impossible to change old ways, to adopt a new communication style. But the more you stick with it, the better you'll get. And the rewards will be obvious. You will probably find that other people are responding to you in healthier, more thoughtful ways, that you and the other person's monsters are not getting in the way as much as they used to, and that you are better able to avoid power struggles that can lead to verbal or physical abuse.

Even if you never manage to change another person's behavior one iota, you can feel pride in knowing that you have done everything possible to make the relationship stronger. You can walk away knowing that you did your best, and that it was the other person's choice not to respond. Remember, don't judge your success as a communicator by what other people say or do, but rather by what YOU are able to say and do. Simply speaking your mind in a thoughtful, open, and assertive way is true success.

42

Forgiveness: the Ultimate Therapy

> No act of kindness,
> no matter how
> small, is ever wasted.
> —*Aesop*

We started this journey of monsters and myths on a note of great pain, and we just ended on a lighter note, a note of humor and understanding. In a sense, that progression reflects the same goal in therapy: transforming painful experiences into something life-affirming. Or at least not letting pain keep you from what you want in life.

However, there is a final step that is also important, and in my view, even greater. Greater in the sense that it can be even more healing. Once you have walked away, broken ties with your abuser, gone into therapy or begun recovery, the next step is to see if you can find it in your heart to forgive.

Some people resist forgiving their abusers because they feel that would let the abuser "win."

They feel that forgiveness is some sort of weakness. Instead, that's just another control struggle.

I remember not too long ago when I brought up the subject of forgiveness with a teenage patient whose father had been abusive to her throughout her childhood, her reaction was intense. She was furious at me for even suggesting that she could ever forgive the man who had "robbed me of my self-esteem," as she put it. My suggestion that forgiveness could be a goal was, for her, premature. I have no idea whether forgiveness will be premature for you too. If the suffering is too raw right now, then you may need to wait awhile before thinking about forgiveness. However, I hope that at some point you will consider it. Not because it's a gift to someone else (the abuser), but because it's a gift to *yourself*.

I feel very strongly that the act of forgiveness benefits you the survivor more than anyone else. It allows you to move ahead with life, unfettered by the abuser. Think about it. Is there anything worse than being preoccupied with someone who hurt you, when that person may be many miles away, may be unaware of what he did, may not know the depth of your hurt, or, cruelly, may not give a damn whether he hurt you or not? This may be the ultimate humiliation a survivor can inflict on herself.

When people have not forgiven, they usually spend a lot of time living in the past, dwelling on their memories, and feeling very angry toward the abuser. In a way, this is like keeping the monster there to beat them up every day. By focusing on the abuser, the survivor repeats the trauma over and over in her mind.

So when you forgive a person, a group, or an entire society, you rise above the abuser. The abuser loses significance in your mind and, in a sense, you win. You give up the monster of bitterness and hatred that has probably added poison and pain to your life.

When you forgive a person, a group, or an entire society, you rise above the abuser.

There is another way in which forgiveness is essential to your healing process.

A 16-year-old girl who attempts suicide periodically told me the following: "When I get angry at other people I take it out on myself. I get so angry I can't take it any more. Then I turn it on myself. I think about how I could have done things differently. I'm so stupid."

This is the monster of self-blame talking. It's a terrible, harsh monster on the shoulder. It can lead to despair, desperation, and even death.

Think of the case of Vincent Foster, President Clinton's associate, who apparently had a strong perfectionistic drive. Many people who knew him speculated that the same perfectionism which led to his professional success made it impossible for him to deal with the setbacks he faced when he first got to Washington. Despite his many other past successes, his loving family, his host of friends and admiring associates, Mr. Foster committed suicide. I didn't know Mr. Foster and so can't say what complex causes led to this tragic act, but I do know from my work with hundreds of suicidal people that perfectionism can be a cause.

The antidote to perfectionism is forgiveness. Forgiveness for the human frailties within yourself and within other people. As I said in the section on self-talk, the way we relate to others usually mirrors the way we talk to ourselves.

So before you can forgive others, before you can forgive your abuser, you first need to forgive yourself. Direct your compassion and empathy like a beam of light to your own soul. Then you will most likely be amazed to discover how much easier it is to direct that loving light toward others.

Remember, you did what you had to do to survive. So forgive yourself.

As an affirmation, try saying this to yourself:

"I forgive myself. I did the best I could. I am in the process of learning new ways to live and to love."

Saying Goodbye to Your Monster

I have learned in my years as a psychiatrist that you can't forgive until you've gotten the pain and rage out of your system.

A couple of years ago, when I attended the talk by Zig Ziglar, one of the best motivational speakers in the United States, at least 2,000 eager sales professionals gathered to hear him talk about how to be more productive.

Instead of giving the standard how-to-improve-your-bottom-line pitch, he talked about how to balance our lives so as to feel more personally fulfilled, regardless of how much we earn or sell.

All of a sudden, he turned to a topic that really piqued my interest. He started talking about abuse, and then made a powerful suggestion for overcoming this kind of terrible pain and suffering. He told us that the key to overcoming one's abusive experiences is to find a way to get the pain out. Then, he said, "Get it out, get it out, and get it out, until you've gotten it all out. Once you've gotten it all out, then forgive." That comment really made an impact on me. I suddenly realized that this is what patients do in psychotherapy. However until that moment, I hadn't grasped that what my patients were finally experiencing was forgiveness. I hadn't really pictured that as the goal. In my entire formal training as a psychiatrist, I had never had a single lecture on forgiveness. Since hearing Zig's wise words, I have talked often with minister friends about this very issue. I have learned that forgiveness has always been central to their ministry and healing. Ah. As I always say to my patients, better to learn late than never. The one "catch" to forgiveness, however, is that it involves some loss. Anger, in a strange way, ties you to another person. It's odd, but true. One person could be in Alaska and the other in Paris, but if they are intensely angry at each other it can feel as if they are still connected, living next door to one another. So when you give up anger, you also give up the tie to your abuser, and if that person was also someone important to you, a parent, sibling, friend, family member, lover, or spouse, then it's likely to feel like a loss. You'll need to give yourself the same time and space to grieve as you would any other loss. It may help to remember that the void you are feeling will leave a space for better, healthier relationships in the future. You can remind yourself that you are in the process of saying goodbye to your monster. Goodbyes hurt. But you're doing it because the monster wasn't a real friend. There are better friends out there, waiting for you once you're ready to embrace them.

As you continue on your journey, you will find other resources to help you. The Resources section of this book provides a list of some of the ones I have found helpful. People close to you may also be good sources of information on articles, books, videos, films, other people, and organizations.

Remember, be patient. I've never met or worked with anyone who's gone from a deep depression, loss, or anger to full recovery of their self-esteem overnight. It takes time. It takes patience with yourself. It takes forgiving yourself for setbacks and for not being perfect. Most of all, it takes faith.

Good luck to you! You're on your way!

Resources

Books

Adams, Kenneth M., Ph.D. *Silently Seduced: When Parents Make Their Children Partners.* (Understanding Covert Incest). Deerfield Beach, FL: Health Communications, 1991.

Bass, E. and Davis, L. *The Courage to Heal: A Guide for Women Survivors of Child Sexual Abuse.* NY: Harper & Row, 1988.

Blanchard, Kenneth, Ph.D., and Spencer Johnson, M.D. *The One Minute Manager.* NY: Berkley, 1982.

Blanchard, Kenneth, Ph.D., William Oncken, and Hal Burrows. *The One Minute Manager Meets the Monkey.* NY: Quill/Morrow, 1989.

Bradshaw, J. *Healing the Shame That Binds You.* Deerfield Beach, FL: Health Communications, 1988.

Burns, David, M.D. *The Feeling Good Handbook.* NY: Morrow, 1989.

Davis, Martha, Ph.D.; Elizabeth Robbins Eshelman, M.S.W.; and Matthew McKay, Ph.D. *The Relaxation and Stress Reduction Workbook.* Oakland, CA: New Harbinger, 1988.

Dawson, Roger. *Power Negotiating.* Chicago, IL: Nightingale Conant, 1987.

Gaylin, Wilard. *Rediscovering Love.* NY: Viking/ Penguin, 1986.

Hendrix, Harville, Ph.D. *Getting the Love You Want: A Guide for Couples.* Harper Perennial/ Harper-Collins, 1988.

Kano, Susan. *Making Peace With Food.* revised edition, Harper & Row, c1989.

Kasl, Charlotte D. *Women, Sex and Addiction: A Search for Love and Power.* NY: Ticknor & Fields, 1989.

Lew, M. *Victims No Longer: Men Recovering from Incest and Other Sexual Child Abuse.* NY: Nevraumont, 1988.

245

Miller, A. *Thou Shalt Not Be Aware: Society's Betrayal of the Child.* NY: Farrar, Strauss & Giroux, 1984.

Milman, Dan. *The Way of the Peaceful Warrior.* Tiburon, CA: H.J. Kramer, 1984.

Norwood, R. *Women Who Love Too Much: When You Keep Wishing and Hoping He'll Change.* NY: Simon & Schuster, 1985.

Osherson, S. *Finding Our Fathers: How a Man's Life Is Shaped by his Relationship with his Father.* NY: Ballantine, 1986.

Peck, M.S. *The Road Less Traveled: A New Psychology of Love, Traditional Values and Spiritual Growth.* NY: Simon & Schuster, 1978.

Roy, Maria. *Children in the Crossfire.* Deerfield Beach, FL: Health Communications, 1988.

Siegel, Bernard. *How to Live Between Office Visits.* NY: Harper & Row.

Siegel, Bernard. *Love, Medicine and Miracles: Lessons Learned About Self-Healing from a Surgeon's Experience with Exceptional Patients.* NY: Harper & Row, 1986.

Tannen, Deborah, Ph.D. *You Just Don't Understand: Women and Men in Conversation.* NY: Ballantine, 1990.

Tannen, Deborah, Ph.D. *That's Not What I Meant! How Conversational Style Makes or Breaks Your Relations with Others.* NY: Morrow, 1986.

Williams, Mary Jane. *Healing Hidden Memories: Recovery for Adult Survivors of Childhood Abuse.* Deerfield Beach, FL: Health Communications, 1990.

Organizations

Incest and Child Abuse
Adults Molested as Children United (AMACU)
P.O. Box 952
San Jose, CA 95108
(408) 280-5055

Incest Survivors Anonymous
P.O. Box 5613
Long Beach, CA 90805
(213) 422-1632

National Child Abuse Hotline
Childhelp USA
P.O. Box 630
Hollywood, CA 90028
(800) 422-4453

Survivors of Incest Anonymous
World Service Office
P.O. Box 21817
Baltimore, MD 21222
(301) 282-3400

Survivors of Incest Gaining Health (SIGH)
20 West Adams, Suite 2015
Chicago, IL 60606

Alcoholism and Substance Abuse
Alcoholics Anonymous World Services (AA)
P.O. Box 459, Grand Central Station
New York, NY 10163
(212) 686-1100

Alcoholics Anonymous –
General Services Office (AA)
468 Park Avenue South
New York, NY 10016
(212) 686-1100

Al-Anon Family Group Headquarters
1372 Broadway, 7th Floor
New York, NY 10018
(800) 245-4656
(212) 302-7240 (NY area)

Children of Alcoholics Foundation
200 Park Avenue, 31st Floor
New York, NY 10166
(212) 949-1404

Narcotics Anonymous World Services Office (NA)
P.O. Box 9999
Van Nuys, CA 91409
(818) 780-3951

National Association for Children of Alcoholics
  (NACOA)
31706 Coast Highway
South Laguna, CA 92677
(714) 499-3889

Overeaters Anonymous – National Office
4025 Spencer Street, Suite 203
Torrance, CA 90504
(213) 542-8363

For Referral to Other Support Groups
National Self-Help Clearinghouse
33 West 42nd Street
New York, NY 10036
(212) 840-1259

About the Author

David J. Schopick, M.D., is a board certified child, adolescent, and adult psychiatrist in private practice and a staff psychiatrist at the Portsmouth Pavilion in Portsmouth, New Hampshire. He earned his M.D. degree from the University of Connecticut, and completed a residency in adult psychiatry at the University of Chicago and the University of Pittsburgh and a fellowship in child and adolescent psychiatry at the University of Pittsburgh.

Currently Dr. Schopick works with children, adolescents, and adults. He has counseled hundreds of people in recovery from verbal, physical, and sexual abuse.

Dr. Schopick is also a popular speaker and workshop leader on such topics as:

Childhood Abuse & Recovery
Childhood & Adult Attention Deficit
    Hyperactivity Disorder
Codependency Communicating Effectively

Communication Problems at Home
Communication Problems at Work
Date/Acquaintance Rape
Dealing with Anger
Forgiveness and Healing
Monsters on the Shoulder
Parent Effectiveness Training
Suicide

For more information about Dr. Schopick's clinical work or workshop series, contact:

Dr. David J. Schopick, M.D.
118 Maplewood Avenue
Portsmouth, NH 03801
(603) 431-5411